BEENY, Sarah

A date with
Sarah Beeny

Sarah Beeny is the presenter of Channel 4's hugely popular Property Ladder and author of several bestselling books; she also writes for The Times and various magazines. A success-ful business woman, Sarah's light-hearted approach and down to earth attitude are reflected in mysinglefriend.com, the website she set up in 2005 with her friend Amanda. Amanda Christie, a web and marketing specialist, was the ideal partner for their venture; and mysinglefriend.com has taken the nation by storm.

With its refreshing new approach to online dating, mysingle-friend.com now has cult status amongst the UK's single pop-ulation.

A Date With
Sarah Beeny

A Date With
Sarah Beeny

mysinglefriend.com's guide to
dating and dumping, flirting and flings

Sarah Beeny
and Amanda Christie

HARPER

HARPER

An Imprint of HarperCollins*Publishers*
77–85 Fulham Palace Road
Hammersmith, London W6 8JB

HarperCollins' website address is:
www.harpercollins.co.uk

Published by HarperCollins*Publishers* 2007

1 3 5 7 9 10 8 6 4 2

A catalogue record for this book is
available from the British Library

ISBN-13 978-0-00-725042-4
ISBN-10 0-00-725042-8

Printed in Great Britain by
Clays Ltd, St Ives plc

With Thanks to...

Andrew Holmes

Laura and Don Barnes

James Barnes

The mysinglefriend.com team: Matt, Shevi, Fred, Naomi, Nick, Emily, Laura, Jon, Clare and Karen

The mysinglefriend.com members who have contributed to this book

All those who have kindly supported mysinglefriend.com

Contents

Introduction

You've probably seen me on telly, bossing people around about the right way to do up their houses. But I don't stop at houses. I'm also prone to bossing people around in their love lives, and there is nothing I like better than to try to give people a shove in the right direction. For years I've been dabbling in matchmaking my pals, encouraged by my more game-on friends. So, going from setting up my friends to setting up a dating website wasn't much of a stretch. Put it this way: nobody was exactly surprised.

The idea came about (like so many ideas do) over a bottle of wine. I'd been getting a little despondent about my matchmaking hobby. The reality is that the older you get, the more difficult it is to meet a partner. More and more people are pairing off; people become more picky (must be a veggie, must support Aston Villa, must chew with mouth closed – that kind of thing); and people go out less and less, being generally happier with a glass of Merlot and repeats of *ER* than crushing up at the bar of their local. As a result it had become increasingly difficult to matchmake my single friends; instead I found myself describing them to each other. It was after one such conversation that I found myself shaking my husband awake at four in the morning to tell him about my new idea.

A website where we all posted details of our single friends.

I think he said, 'Ugh,' or it could have been, 'Ach,' and then he put a pillow over his head. This was quite good for him. Normally he just swears. Result.

Next day, I phoned Amanda.

I should introduce Amanda Christie, my partner in crime – not only in the website but in this book, too. What Amanda doesn't know about dating either isn't worth knowing or is illegal. She's also my oldest friend and my son's godmother.

Plus... she has a company building websites with her husband, James. I suggested the site and a few days later she phoned back and said, 'Let's go for it.'

We decided they would build it and run it and I would make sure everyone knew about it. It took James and Amanda a year to build the site with the help of an IT wiz, Matt, who now works for the site full-time.

In August 2005 we launched mysinglefriend.com. I say 'launched'. In actual fact, we put about eight single friends on it and rang everyone we knew, begging them to put their single friends on it, too. Finding the first 100 people was like getting blood out of a stone. I don't blame them. After all, it was a leap of faith. But it grew, slowly at first, then picked up, and now we're one of the most popular dating sites in the UK.

So, why do a book? Because the philosophy of mysingle-friend.com has always been that dating should mean good times, not bad ones. We engineered the site based on those values, and found that we were one of the few sites to do so. Then, looking around at dating books, we found a similar problem: none of them seemed to acknowledge the sheer enjoyment of dating – whether it's choosing who you want to hook up with, going on the date itself or the funny anecdotes you have to tell the day after. Of course, we're not advocating that you treat the process like a joke, but we believe that you won't get the best out of it unless you have a good time.

Why? Because you owe it to yourself, that's why. Because if you're single, what you don't realize is that you're the envy of almost every couple on the planet. All those people you admire for being so happy. Sure, they *are* happy, but you know what they miss? The thrill of those first few dates, the excitement of getting to know someone else, that indescribably great feeling you get when it all seems to click. And, yes, that fortnight you spend in bed.

So we're not here to help you in a mad dash up the aisle. We're here to help you get the most out of your single life, And, hell, by the end of this book you never know – you may well end up with Mr or Ms Right, if that's what you're after.

And while we're at it, we decided to throw in a whole bunch of helpful hints about how to get a date, what to wear, how to flirt, how to prepare for your date, how to dump and get dumped, and so on and so on...

Plus, we thought we'd have a really good laugh doing it. Here's hoping you enjoy taking our advice as much as we enjoyed giving it. Oh, and remember one thing...

We're *dead* jealous!

Chapter One

So You're Single?

well, you're not alone

Being single is a living nightmare. Every evening, in cockroach-infested bedsits all over the country, single people grimly clear away the remains of their meal-for-one, tearfully wash the one wine glass they've been using to drown their sorrows, and get into their cold, empty, single beds before ramming fistfuls of Nytol down their throats, hoping against hope that tonight they will be able to sleep, and for a few blissful hours at least, the bleak reality of their meaningless single existence will cease its slow, agonizing torture.

That's what people in relationships like to think, anyway. At mysinglefriend.com we know that the reality is entirely different. Sorry, People-in-Relationships, but being single is not a disease. It does not warrant your pity. It is not a state of mind. In fact, it's brilliant, and it beats being in an unhappy relationship hands down.

Being unattached doesn't mean you're unhappy or unfulfilled. It just means you haven't met someone who makes you as happy – or happier – than you are on your own, and on whom you have the same effect.

First, remember that you don't *have* to be single. You could be with someone by this afternoon if you wanted to; it's just that you're not prepared to lower your standards that far. Why? Because doing so would mean a lifetime of drudgery with someone who bugs the hell out of you, that's why. And if that sounds like common sense then that's because it is. Still, you'd be surprised at the amount of people who are in relationships not because of the happiness equation, not because they're in love or even for more noble reasons like 'the children', but simply because they were so scared of being alone that they grasped at whatever specimen was the first to show an iota of interest. These are the people you hear through the walls at night, chucking stuff at one another. They go to bed after another evening of crockery flinging and you can bet your life they're *desperately* wishing they were single. They're wishing they were you right now.

So, one thing this book definitely *isn't* about is racing to shed your singleness, like it's a paper coat that just caught fire. It's about having fun finding not just *any* old partner but a good one. Even so, while being single should be the most fun time imaginable, there will come a time when you begin to wonder if you might be having more (or different) fun if you were with somebody. There are times when you begin to wonder if you really are single through choice. This is when the blues kick in. And if you're single and looking for love, they can be your worst enemy. What are they?

1. 'Love Has Passed Me By!'

It's deadly to fall into the trap of thinking you're an unloveable wretch, unworthy of a partner's attention. Perhaps you've been bruised by one too many bad relationships, or a succession of bad dates has left you thinking that it's you at fault, not your date. You begin to feel like a romantic loser. Who would want a klutz like you anyway?

- **You need to change your way of thinking** Sure, the love bomb hasn't dropped yet but it will. What's suffocating the process is you thinking that dating is bound to end in disaster. It's all about placing a high price on yourself and having a glass-half-full attitude when it comes to meeting potential partners. Let's face it: if you're sitting on the other side of the dinner table with a face like your dog's died, your date will be checking their watch and mentally running through a list of get-out-quick excuses. (Big meeting tomorrow. Sudden stomach cramps. Previously undiagnosed allergy to garlic bread.) Yes, this date might go south along with your 10 previous dates but so what if it does? You had a laugh, didn't you? You've got some stories to tell your friends and you've met some really great people/really odd people/borderline psychotics (delete as applicable).

2. 'I'm a Professional Singleton'

Again, it's a trap you can't help but fall into. You start dividing the world into 'couples' and 'singles'. Instead of seeing people as people you define them by their relationships. It's a sign that you're too hung up on your single status, frankly, and ditching that attitude would be a very helpful thing to do.

- **So be 'you', not the token single person** Because you don't want other people to start seeing you solely in terms of your single status either. It ends up being a handicap. Don't forever bang on about being on your own. Before you know it, your whole life will be geared towards finding a partner, and that is the best way to not find a partner. Nothing is more off-putting than a desperate single.

3. 'I Always End Up with the Wrong Type'

Your last four relationships have been disasters because he or she was a wrong-un. Your friends have started calling you the Bad Boy Junkie or the Bitch Magnet, and you're feeling pretty disillusioned with the opposite sex right now. They always let you down. They're never faithful. All they do is nag and criticize…

- **You deserve better** If you think you're doomed to fall in love with wrong-uns, then you will because you're putting a low price on yourself. Loyal and reliable doesn't mean boring and predictable; it just means that you're getting the respect you deserve.

4. 'I've Built Walls'

A little story. A friend of ours met a woman at a party and asked what she did for a living. 'Why?' the woman snapped back. 'Why do people have to be judged by what they do for a living?' Hey, it was just a question, just a conversational opener at a party. Needless to say, our friend scarpered. For whatever reason, this woman had built some pretty big walls around herself – had 'issues' of some kind – and as a result was scaring people away. Literally.

- **Knock them down** Snapping at a fellow party guest is no way to start a conversation, is it? Scowling at someone when they accidentally put their foot in it isn't going to score you points for great social skills. Yes, the details of small talk can sometimes seem trivial or shallow, and yes, it's painfully hard work talking to people you have nothing in common with, but don't get bitter and defensive. Talk to people.

5. 'I Scare Partners Off'

A typical dating cycle sees you meeting someone tasty and you seem to get on, but after two or three dates they're cooling off, then they stop returning your calls and, before you know it, you're history. *Again*. Now you're starting to wonder why you even bothered in the first place.

- **So learn from your experiences** Like anything else, good dating takes practice, and perhaps you need a bit more. Or maybe you're committing one of these dating faux pas...

- **You've mistaken 'new love' for 'new partner'** In other words, you've gone too far too quickly. Probably the most common error at the beginning of relationships is for one partner to assume that the romance is something it's not. Some people like to jump head first into domestic bliss 24/7; for other people it's their idea of hell, and misjudging that can be fatal. One of you will come off looking insecure and needy; the other will begin to pull away, which only makes the insecure one even *more* needy and insecure. Before you know it, one of you is driving past the other's house at two in the morning. Ouch.

However tempting it is to hereby declare this relationship well and truly open, don't. Just because you've slept with someone, or had a handful of great dates, doesn't suddenly give you the right to know where they were last night, or expect them to be changing their weekend plans to include you.

- **You got too complacent too quickly** Once again it's all too common for people to start a relationship then assume it will take care of itself. Sorry, but it won't. It's not just a box you can tick, like a pension, life cover, or an umbrella in case it rains. If somebody feels they've simply been slotted into an empty compartment in another person's life they will be resentful. So keep some of the best of you for them, and give the relationship all the attention you can – otherwise that box is going to get unticked again pretty sharpish.

- **You've always got to be top dog** Could it be that in your bid to show your new beau how totally money you are, you end up going over the top? You'd hardly be the first. An ultra-common new relationship complaint is for one partner to get sick of the other's endless boasting. Hand in hand with that goes the tendency to always be right. No one likes a smarty-pants; nobody likes someone constantly blowing their own trumpet and – news flash – it's not a sign of weakness to admit that you're wrong every now and again.

Just remember that feeling good about your single life means feeling good about yourself. If you're falling into any of the traps above, then you're likely to find yourself in a vicious circle of no dates and bad dates – and that's when it gets too much like hard work. Relax. Stop being so hard on yourself. Stop thinking every date's going to be a disaster and get out there to meet new people. But what if one of your dating blues is...

6. 'I Never Meet Anyone New!'

Then read on...

Chapter Two

Lingering Looks at the Deli Counter

the supermarket, and other places to pull

Technically speaking, the Pet Shop Boys were bang on the money when they sang 'Love Comes Quickly'. It certainly does. The problem is, getting it into bed in the first place. And this is where the tricky question of meeting those all-important dates comes in. Just where do you go to bump into Mr Right or Ms Right, or even just Mr Mainly-Right-at-Weekends? And what do you do if and when bumping occurs? Relax, we've got the seven-day solution to your meet-market woes...

Monday: You Do the Food Shopping

Let's be honest here – the chance meeting in the supermarket is the kind of thing that only really happens in romantic comedies. In Film World, beautiful singles' hands will meet while both reaching for the last bottle of Pinot. They'll strike up clever (but sexy) repartee, get together, split up then get back together again. Roll credits.

In real life, however, supermarkets are bleak cathedrals of pain, full of drones on little more than autopilot, ruthlessly hacking each other down in the rush for the shortest queue and murderously muttering, 'That's never 10 items,' at the express till.

Nevertheless, it *can* happen. You catch someone's eye in a supermarket, and you subconsciously have that 'hot or not' moment. If they are staring back at you and they're not hot, or have about 20 years on you, you will probably automatically assume it's because they know your dad, or that you need to wipe your nose. However, if they *are* hot, your age, and don't have another half obviously in tow, there has to be a way to try and take things a little further – and there is…

Aisle Be Back

Just because you're in the supermarket at half past three on a Monday afternoon doesn't mean you can't have that 'eyes across the dance floor' moment. Assuming you don't actually have a bogey hanging out of your nose, you've checked and you're looking half-decent, then how do you make contact? A surreptitious check of their trolley is a good start. If it's stuffed with the dreaded meals-for-one and a copy of this book, then keep those lingering looks going and make sure you choose the same queue at the checkout. If it's Pampers and packets of breast pads, one word: eek.

✓ **Also try:** A book shop, the library, the train, an art gallery – all those other 'movie' places.

? **Success-o-meter:** A lowly two out of ten, unless you're Jennifer Aniston, Matthew McConaughey, etc...

Tuesday:
You're at Work

Check out the figures: 87 per cent of couples in London met through work or started dating at work, and 60 per cent of the country's workforce has had some kind of office orifice-action during their career. It doesn't take a genius to work out why. In some ways your work colleagues know you better than your own family – you certainly spend more time with them. They met you with few preconceptions, so you are (as far as anyone can be) 'yourself'. At the very least you have work in common with them, they live near you, will probably be of a similar age and you *know* whether they're married or not. Bingo.

Downsides? Yes. Some companies don't allow it, so you need to be prepared to leave your dream job if that work fling comes skipping over the horizon. Plus, you'll be distracted, work longer hours, spend more cash on clothes and probably have the slow-roasting agony of not knowing whether your crush feels the same way.

Office Politics

You'll no doubt have an inkling whether the person you like fancies you too. That's because we learnt all this stuff in the playground. Remember at school the person who made jokes about you and made you squirm? They were paying you attention, and that's because they 'really, really liked' you. Work is not terribly different, so look out for the play-ground signs:

1. They catch your eye (knowing glances, rolling of eyes, winks and smiles).

2. They try to prolong contact with you (like emailing or calling you when it isn't really necessary).

3. They ask questions about your personal life (but remember, 'What are

you doing tonight?' does not always beg the reply, 'Having a drink with you.').

4. They bring you stuff (even a cup of coffee or something from the stationery cupboard scores points here).

5. They try to make you laugh.

When it comes to getting it together, there's always that old standby, the company party. Getting 'tipsy' is the easiest way to make a fool of yourself *and* brush it off the next day. If you don't have one of those pencilled in until the next millennium, then you need to try and engineer a drink together. Go for the matey, 'Hey, fancy a drink after work tonight?' rather than the more datey (and scary), 'Would you like to go out one night?' That way, nobody's dignity gets shredded if your affections aren't reciprocated. But go for it – nothing will come of this crushing crush until you get some time together. If your approach doesn't work, well, you tried. Next!

Once you're in there, so to speak, behave discreetly. Providing you don't tell everyone, or start smooching by the water cooler, you should be free to enjoy the very guilty pleasure of dating at work – plus you've saved yourself some petrol money in the process. Nice one.

One last thing on workplace dating. What if one of you is the boss? If you're the person in charge, it's a tricky one;

sometimes you just have to be the bad guy in the office. This does not necessarily make you off-limits to the opposite sex (in fact, sometimes it adds to the excitement) but be careful about making the first move here – you can make it known with some playground signs of your own that an advance would not be unwelcome.

If you're the underling, meanwhile, do not assume you will get a promotion by tupping your boss. Sorry, not a chance.

✓ **Also try:** Evening classes, self-defence, am-dram, a book group, AA meetings – places where love 'flowers', in other words...

? **Success-o-meter:** Got to be a hefty eight out of ten. Statistically speaking, you're most likely to end up with someone from work.

Wednesday: You Hit the Bar with Some Friends

Okay, so a huge amount depends on what sort of 'bar' you're hitting. The snug of the Red Cow during Morris Dancing Week? Or happy hour in All Bar One? All they really have in common is booze, crisps and a small window in the lavatories. Still, most of us tend to think of bars, whatever their stripe, as being good places to meet people. But are they really? In fact, they flatter to deceive, and the usual extensive research (of asking our friends) reveals that almost nobody starts a fling in a bar – not unless they're introduced by a pal. The trouble is that groups of people tend to arrive at bars then leave together, and don't mingle much in between. Yes, there's always chucking-out time, but do you really want to start a relationship with a glassy-eyed soak whose opening line is, 'You'll do...'?

Bar Talk

If you've got the bottle to go up to a group of strangers and introduce yourself to the fittest person there, then you've had enough to drink, and in fact you've probably just started a conversation with a fruit machine. No, going to the bar is pretty much your only option if you want to get chatting to someone new.

On the upside, people like to exchange pleasantries at the bar, even if it's just to moan about the staff. The disadvantage is that you have to be super quick or, as you're standing there debating how to open proceedings, they'll be turning away to rejoin their mates. Get in there. Chance it with a bit of small talk, not a really naff line like, 'Do you come here often?' Try something like, 'Aren't you John's friend?' (obviously you don't actually have to have a friend called John). Hopefully you'll know if there is a spark.

✓ **Also try:** Walking the dog, a football match, the gym, the coffee shop (where your eyes can meet while searching for a spare copy of the *Guardian* or spraying each other with sugar from the sachets or accidentally putting cinnamon on your grande latte cappy-frappy-mochaccino instead of chocolate – ew).

? **Success-o-meter:** A cautious five for this one.

Thursday: You Go to Lucy's 'I'm Having a Year Off' Party
(the jammy thing!)

Ah, almost the perfect meeting place. You're there because you know X and they know Y, who just happens to know rather gorgeous Z standing by the French doors. One or two introductions later, you get talking, you hit it off and S is meeting E and X. Result. In fact, the only downside of a party is that everybody gets smashed too quickly, so take it easy on the pop, work the room and get chatting.

Party Animal

Once you find yourself talking to the object of your lust, there's only really one opener: 'How do you know [insert name of party organizer here]?' On the face of it you're simply asking how they know the host or hostess. But what you're *really* asking is, 'Are you attached?' Fit person knows this, and if they've got a partner in the wings, they'll refer to them in their reply. That is, unless they're stupid.

✓ **Also try:** Other parties! If there's a house to be warmed, an engagement to be toasted, a birthday to celebrate, you're there. Oh, and wakes, too. They're uncommonly good places to pull, weirdly enough.

? **Success-o-meter:** A meaty seven for this one.

Friday: You Put On Your Dancing Shoes

There are only two reasons people go to clubs. One is to take drugs and dance to records that all sound the same. The other is to get seriously flirty. Unlike bars, where mates tend to stick together, the darkness and after-hours buzz of a club is where people go for it. Which is all good, except this probably isn't the place to come if you're looking for anything beyond a reason to remove your underwear.

Club Together

Most of the proper flirting gets done on the dance floor, so, sorry, but you're going to have to bust some moves. Chances are, if things progress, you'll end up moving off the dance floor and either to the bar or to a quieter part of the club. Go with the flow, but here's a tip: don't give out your number – take theirs. You'll thank us for that in the morning.

✓ **Also try:** A concert, a festival, another club...

? **Success-o-meter:** Four for long-term loving. Seven for short-term shagging.

Saturday: It's Tom and Geri's Wedding, and You're Invited

Tradition dictates that weddings are the best place to meet your future spouse. Presumably this is because weddings are heaving with friends-of-friends, sexy brothers and sisters and 'Hey, how come you never mentioned your cousin was so fit?'

types – which just goes to show that the perfect person is often closer than you think. What's more, the champagne is flowing, everybody's smartly dressed and every non-attached person there is walking around with raging hormones for the day.

Things to beware of, though. First, you're drunk. If you're at a wedding and you're not a little bit squiffy then the chances are you've just conducted the ceremony. Second, your friends and family are all there, and they will be watching as you use your tongue for tonsil-probes on the dance floor. Do you want your nearest and dearest to see you act like a 14-year-old? It's not a good look.

Vow Factor

Meeting somebody at a wedding is as easy as falling off a Vaseline-coated log in the rain – while wearing flip-flops. For a start, you've got a whole day to do it. Then, the organizers practically force you to sit next to people of the opposite sex whom you don't know. You all get drunk. You all have something to talk about. Everybody knows someone who can make an introduction. You get handed drinks, have a boogie and sit at a table giggling at all the dad-dancers. Still, don't assume that you can sit by yourself looking mysterious and the best-looking guest in the place will come and hunt you out – get some champers down you and go for it.

Also try: Friends of friends.

Success-o-meter: A six if you're invited to the reception only, rising to an eight if you're there for the whole day.

Sunday: You Go on Your Hols

Holiday romances are just that – very romantic. You have the luxury of getting to know somebody properly, except the whole process is hothoused to the duration of a (very sexy) fortnight. Skiing trips, in particular, seem to be a great opportunity for this, especially if someone skis like a god. Most people are there with mates so they're out to have a laugh. Plus, if the person you've got your eye on is part of a couple, chances are they'll be there together, so you won't get caught out chatting up someone who then introduces you to their other half.

On the other side of the euro, holiday romances are almost always doomed to failure. You live in London; they live in the Hebrides. Or, worse, you live in Bristol and they're a Masai tribesman. Be cautious of giving out your details. If Helios from the taverna turns up at the PR company you work for, complete with tight bathing shorts, halting English and grand plans to emigrate, you've got yourself a big, fat Greek problem. Taking holiday romances home is a disaster – leave them there.

Sun Kissed

On holiday you have almost every conceivable social occasion in your lap, only with the advantage of no domestic worries whatsoever. As with the work fling you can afford to take your time – but don't hang about too much.

✓ **Also try:** Sorry, but there isn't really an alternative to the holiday romance, which is why they're simultaneously special and fraught.

? **Success-o-meter:** Seven if you're after the quick-fix fumble, but a shoddy one if it's lasting results you require.

So finding a date is simple? No, not really. And what do you do if you struggle to strike up conversations with total strangers, don't drink, work from home and do all your supermarket shopping online? Well, then you have to look elsewhere...

Chapter Three

GSOH, Must Have Own Axe

the scary, fun and fabulous world of dating agencies

The days when you'd sooner wake up naked and locked out of your house than join a dating agency are history. And that's because we've finally accepted that society has moved on.

Yes, gone are the times when gentlefolk got chatting while buying candles in Arkwrights on Monday, then were married a week Saturday.

Now we have online shopping.

During the war, thousands of people met in underground air-raid shelters, spending what might have been their final evenings on this earth 'getting to know each other'.

Now we have 'Tube rage'. Depressing, isn't it? We've become a nation of isolationists.

So, in the same way that millions of years ago humans learnt to walk on two legs in order to best cope with the demands of their environment, now we have evolved dating agencies – in order to best cope with the demands of ours. There are lots of them. They're scary. They're rarely light on the wallet. But if you're looking for love (or even just a little bit of lust), the chances are you might find one that works for you.

There's internet dating, which, obviously, we think is fun and accessible, and we know works (cough). But let's be fair. There's also speed dating (for the impatient); lunch-break dating (for the hungry); supper dating (for the hungrier); dating in the dark (for those who don't consider the light 'a friend'); karaoke dating (for budding singers); silent dating (for the quiet); orgy dating (for the horny). And probably speed, lunch, orgy, karaoke dating in the dark.

There are niche markets too: music, wine, art, gardening, horoscopes, single parents, literary, cuisine, gothic, bondage, yellow trousers, you name it. If there's a magazine for it, there's a dating option, too. Don't be too dazzled by a niche market agency though – opposites attract. Plus it's cool to meet people who have an interest outside of train sets...

First, Though, Some General Tips...

- **Stay in control.** Make sure it's *you* doing the choosing, not some computer or a woman in an office on Kilburn High Road. Only you can choose who you might like to date.

- **Never join a dating agency without seeing what's on offer.** You wouldn't join a book club without seeing the books, would you? If the agency has some spurious reason why you can't see the potential dates in advance, then you're about to get taken for a ride. Alert, alert. Grab your skirts and run.

- **When you've decided to go for it – join with a friend.** A pal around to remind you who you are and why you are doing this can be a great support. You can laugh about it together too.

- **Ask for recommendations from the agency in question – if they can't deliver, move on.** If you feel you are being patronized or fobbed off, move on. Ask how many members they've got – you need to know what kind of dating pool you're joining.

Speed Dating

What Is It?

They said it was a gimmick that would never last – and they were half right. In fact, this US export has proved remarkably popular in the UK, and though our usual rigorous research method of relying on anecdotal evidence from friends says that it doesn't score well in the perfect-partner stakes, those who take part are having a whale of a time. Not exactly the most romantic way to meet your one true love, it works by having the ladies sit at tables and the men moving among them. Each pair spends a torturous (or, hopefully, transcendental) three minutes together before a bell, buzzer or a farty sound goes, and the man moves on to the next table. Repeat till fade. You're given a card and pen, and it's up to you to keep track of who's impressed you, putting a tick by their name if you fancy seeing them again. At the end of the night you hand in the card and organizers match the ticks so interested parties can get in touch with each other. Sounds exhausting, doesn't it?

What Do I Do?

Get some info up front. Ask for the numbers and age groups. Where do they advertise? What kind of repeat business do they get? Is the evening always full?

Once you take the plunge and go along – go for it. Timid Tracy never nibbled nervous Neil or vice versa. Ah, but what if you can't think of anything to say? There's a trick to this: the more you think the less you say. Imagine they were a friend or colleague and you were chit-chatting – they will immediately feel at home in your company. They will be asked by at least five other people (who think they are being terribly droll) whether they have done this sort of thing before, and oh, isn't it embarrassing. Sod the pleasantries; if you like them, try and find out what they like.

The more you think the less you say, but the more you drink the more you say. A tipple or two can be favourable for the nerves, but turn tipsy to 'totalled' and you're boozy and boring.

But what to do if you are feeling confident and have tried the above but your prospective paramour is not taking the date bait? You try and discover their interests and they mumble the odd word while their eyes wander the room like marbles on a work surface? They are either not interested or boring. Logic tells us from previous relationships that dating someone who is either boring or not interested in you can be drawn out and painful, like stubbing your toe. Move on.

How Should I Prepare?

Just the one glass of wine, no more. And when you're getting ready for a speed-date event, remember that first impressions really count here, so bear that puppy in mind. It's no good wearing your 'ironic' Iron Maiden T-shirt because the chances are your date won't get it, and they'll go away thinking you're into hair metal. And that's not a good look.

How Do You Rate My Chances?

Hey, can't be bad. You've got a potential 30 dates in one night.

Dating in the Dark

What Is It?

It's a blind date. Literally. A group of you sit at dinner, *in the dark*, while you're served by waiters wearing night-vision goggles (you know, the sort used by serial killers).

What Do I Do?

The idea is that, unable to see, your other senses – smell, taste, hearing, touch – are heightened and you'll fall desperately in love with the silky tones of the person opposite. Except, of course, the lights go up and you discover that not only are they a minger but they've been sitting there cracking one off while you've been discussing the salmon.

How Should I Prepare?

Er, eat carrots?

How Do You Rate My Chances?

Not high. Low, in fact. Frankly, dating in the dark is only worth a punt if you want to have a bit of a giggle – and you don't care about beetroot juice staining your white shirt.

Lunch-break Dating

What Is It?

Single people are always very busy, have you noticed? Always 'too busy' to meet other people (hence dating agencies), 'too busy' to go on proper dates (hence speed dating) and now 'too busy' to meet for a proper dinner, like civilized people, hence a 'lunch-break date'.

What Do I Do?

These dating agencies work like any other, except that they arrange dates in your lunch break. Presumably, you grab a sandwich together, spend 20 minutes glancing surreptitiously at your watch, then hurry back to the office and get on with the important business of being really, really busy.

How Should I Prepare?

By struggling into work, staring blankly at a computer screen for hours while drinking countless cups of coffee and trying to ignore your colleagues discussing Celebrity Something or Other. Always the best way to prepare for a date.

How Do You Rate My Chances?

Low. Any 'day date' smells a bit of 'I can't be bothered to invest in this exercise', and these clubs are a depressing sign of the times. Do you really want to reduce life to some kind of boxy, convenient timeslot that fits around your work patterns? Do you? If you ask us, you might as well march straight to the crematorium...

Singles Nights

What Are They?

The term 'singles night' covers a multitude (and we mean *multitude*) of sins. It could be a small party organized by a pal hoping to bring mutual but otherwise unconnected friends together. It could be a bit of a knees-up at your local. It could be a ginormous event of thousands of people set up by a dating agency – at Wembley.

What Do I Do?

Well, you go along. There will no doubt be dancing and booze, and in most respects it'll be just like any other night out *except* you know that everybody is single.

How Should I Prepare?

By playing 'Daydream Believer' by The Monkees shortly before you leave home. If that doesn't give you a spring in your step, nothing will. Trust us – that's a solid-gold tip.

How Do You Rate My Chances?

Meejum. It really does depend on the kind of event you end up going to. Use your considerable nous, choose wisely and you never know...

Classified Ads

What Are They?

It's old-skool dating, and the origin of all that stuff about having a GSOH and being a tall, solvent non-smoker – even if you're a humourless dwarf chaining B&H in front of daytime telly. Frankly, the classified ads are the reason why there was ever a stigma about the dating-agency route of finding a partner in the first place. Why? Because people lied their arses off in order to get a quick shag, that's why. They've been rendered more or less obsolete by online dating, but even so, people still use them.

What Do I Do?

Asking yourself who's still using the classifieds and why would be a good start. People who lack the mental dexterity required to operate a computer, perhaps? Those who like seeing themselves in print? Wanted criminals? If you still think the personal ads are for you, then refer to our handy cut-out-and-keep dating guidelines in the chapter for general advice, but don't say we didn't warn you.

How Do You Rate My Chances?

Ten years ago, we would have said you might end up with a nutter. These days you might end up with a nutter who can't use a PC.

Now, let's see. Is there any kind of dating agency that we've missed...?

Chapter Four

'I'm on the Interweb...'

getting online with mysinglefriend.com and other online agencies

Once upon a time, the online dating world seemed to be full of balding middle-aged men. Now it's positively crammed with cultured, incredibly good-looking and talented people. We know; we're partly responsible for making it that way. If you haven't taken the plunge, believe us – there's never been a better time. And if you need a helping hand? Well, read on.

But first, safety. Or, to put it another way...

Safety First

You wouldn't take someone you'd never met before back to your home, would you? Neither would you introduce Sammy Stranger to your children. And you're not in the practice of shagging people you've just met in Sainsbury's (hopefully).

So don't do it online. Believe it or not, at mysinglefriend.com we get reports of people organizing dates at their workplace (which is dumb) or their home (which is *really* dumb). Why? Well, remember what your mum told you about strangers? Even if you've been chatting to your date on the phone or via email beforehand that doesn't mean you can trust them…

Watch what you put in your profile, too. At mysinglefriend we often have to blitz the following no-nos from people's profiles:

Blitz! 'I always go to such-and-such pub. Always!'

Blitz! 'My kids go to such-and-such school.' (We don't even allow kids' ages, in fact. Sign of the times, but there you go.)

Blitz! 'I work for such-and-such company – in block B, on the third floor, opposite a guy called Graham.'

Blitz! 'You may have seen my dad on TV! He used to be in such-and-such a band.'

Blitz! 'I always go to such-and-such gym, on Tuesday lunchtimes.'

Frankly, you might as well advertise that you enjoy lone walks on Hampstead Heath every Friday night, wearing crotchless knickers. Incidentally, if you're with an agency that doesn't delete this kind of stuff like we do (and most don't), then they're not looking out for you – you might want to think again.

Say Cheese
(yes, the dreaded photo)

Like it or not, your mugshot is going to make or break the experience. Yes it is. And that's not necessarily because people are 'lookist' (we said 'not *necessarily*'), it's because a happy, smiley photo of your face is what people need and want to see. We read so much from a face, especially from the eyes. Remember, you don't have to look like Scarlett Johansson/George Clooney [delete as applicable]. You just need to look like you.

So, the photo where you are climbing Mount Everest may well show off your adventurous side, but you're a pinprick in the distance and no one can see what you look like. Ditch it!

That old, treasured railcard photo – scratched and grainy. You think it makes you look serious and intellectual and, yes, if you're honest, quite a bit younger. Ah, but does it really? Are you sure it doesn't make you look as though you've just been arrested on suspicion of bothering farm animals? Ditch it!

In a lead-lined sealed vault at mysinglefriend.com, we really do have examples of the following...

Compositional Cock-ups

1. **Woman on sofa; pile of ironing behind her.**
   Cock-up: Ironing is the international symbol of something boring, dutiful and drudgy. You might as well pose wearing washing-up gloves, holding a bottle of Domestos in one hand and a packet of Bird's Eye Menu Masters in the other.
   Lesson: Watch out for potentially soul-destroying household items in the background. You'd be surprised how many Hoovers we get to see, for example.

2. **Man on bed, with samurai swords and *Star Wars* wallpaper on the wall.**
   Cock-up: What you're doing there is what we experts call 'foregrounding'. In this case you're foregrounding your interests. Foregrounding is always bad, because ideally you want your date to find out about you in a natural and organic way, not from potentially misleading pieces of information gleaned from a photograph. In this particular case, you're foregrounding an interest in *Star*

Wars, which indicates… Well, it indicates that you like *Star Wars*, for one thing.

Lesson: Look, if you want to meet someone who shares your passionate love affair with *Star Wars*, we're guessing there are *Star Wars* websites, *Star Wars* conventions, stuff like that. That's where you'll find a fellow *Star Wars*-fan. Not on a dating site. So, in a nutshell: don't foreground.

3. **Woman skiing with Balaclava hat on.**

   Cock-up: We can't see your face, love.

   Lesson: (Sigh.)

4. **Face with arm strangely held in the air.**

   Cock-up: A common cock-up this. You've taken a picture of yourself on your camera-phone, haven't you? This gives off two potentially negative messages: 1) you simply can't be arsed to dig out a decent picture of yourself; and 2) you have no friends.

   Lesson: Don't look lonely. Don't look like you don't give a damn about the whole thing. Make a bit of effort, for pity's sake.

5. **Man on a street holding a tin of Fosters.**

   Cock-up: You look like a man on a street holding a tin of Fosters.

   Lesson: We shouldn't really need to tell you this, but

just in case: a man on a street holding a tin of Fosters is Not a Good Look.

6. **Man lying on a bed naked from the waist up.**

Cock-up: You look as though I'm going to wake up in the middle of the night and find you standing over me with a steak knife. Either that or you're going to be bothering me for sex from the moment I order my prawn cocktail.

Lesson: Unless you actually *want* to look like Fred West, keep the clobber on.

7. **Woman smiling (slightly desperately) dressed in a caftan and surrounded by cats.**

Cock-up: You've decided that you looked ace in the 1970s, so you've gone to the box marked 'pictures of me looking ace in the 1970s' and pulled out your favourite one. It also reminds you of Tiddles, your beloved cat, God rest his soul.

Lesson: Recent pics only, please, and remember that just because a photograph has really great associations for you, it doesn't mean they'll come across to the casual browser. You're thinking, 'Oh yes, they will. Tiddles was such a special cat.' Take it from us, they won't.

So, what *do* you do? First, check the surroundings and background of your photo. Does it look interesting to you? A sunny, leafy glade in the background will work better than a poorly lit office wall. Make your photo appealing in all senses, from your smile to what you are wearing.

Write Here, Write Now
(or what your profile says about you)

Put simply, wit wins every time. Not everyone can pen amusing nuggets with the flair of Oscar Wilde, though, so if you can't think of something funny, make it interesting – but most of all, make it unique.

For guidance, here's the ugly, the bad and the good of online profiles.

The Ugly

Nothing is more off-putting than bad writing. Sure, da teens R talkin txt & thts GR8, LOL! ;), but unless you want to go out with a mobile phone, it's not going to look good in your profile – you'll look like you can't even speak, let alone spell.

Ah, yes, spelling. Is it important? Sorry, but yes. Once again, it's not the mistake that's important; it's what it says about you: that you can't be bothered to get it right. Believe it or not, our most common typo at mysinglefriend.com is the word 'intelligent'. Yes, she really is looking for an intellagiant man. Second to having 'inteliginse', she would like you to know that she is 'independant' and reads the 'Indypendent'.

You're on a computer, yes? So whizz your profile through a spellchecker. While you're at it, dump the text-speak (like lol, gsoh, lmao and ttfn), and ditch the five exclamation marks after anything you find funny – it's the prose equivalent of someone giving you a nasty dig in the ribs after they've told you a joke. Not good.

Delving once again into the vaults of mysinglefriend.com, we bring you these absolutely genuine typos…

- 'She has a grounded opinion on most things but would never force an onion on someone else.' **(although has been known to impose other vegetables on her guests)**
- 'I like whining and dining.' **(she's a restaurant critic?)**
- 'I'm an accomplished painist.' **(and has a history of violins)**
- 'I'm a Cornish girl rat heart.' **(but her other internal organs are her own)**
- 'She hates men who email with v bad grammer.' **(especially when they criticize her speling)**
- 'She is highly accademick.' **(i.e. she's good at P.E.)**
- 'She is slim and curry all at the same time.' **(not for long if she keeps that up)**
- 'There's never a dull movement!' **(lots of laughs when they go sit-downs)**

- 'The man has a heart of gold, the patients of a saint and the ability to make anyone smile.' **(he's a doctor, no, he's a clown...)**

- 'I live with the most wonderful dog in the world – photo of Fanny can be supplied.' **(just don't ask about the pussy, okay?)**

The Bad

Now you've mastered the spelling, it's time to get the wording of your profile right. Here are some good examples of what NOT to write...

> 'She likes to curl up with a bottle of wine and a DVD. Equally she likes to party.'

A bit woolly, this. Plus, almost every profile says something similar to it, and you don't want to be one of the herd, do you?

> 'What can I say?' and 'And at the end of the day'

Two of the most-used terms in profiles. Both are entirely meaningless and exhibit an astounding lack of imagination.

> 'I want commitment from a solvent man.

> I don't want a sex pest. My ex has left
> me bruised and lonely. Don't mess me
> around. My confidence can't take it.'

Can you hear that sound? That's the sound of people running in the opposite direction. Too needy! Too much information much too early on!

The Good

Keep it short and sweet – likes and dislikes is a good gauge of how you think, and is an easy way to add wit to a profile. For example:

> **Likes:** chewy sweeties, clean sheets,
> the bit when someone wins an Olympic
> medal.
>
> **Dislikes:** open sandwiches, flavoured
> mayonnaise, the wet spongy bit in a trifle.

Or, what about your six perfect dinner guests?

> **Stephen Fry** (to talk to)
> **Cat Deeley** (to gaze upon)
> **Winston Churchill** (so everyone can smoke)
> **Jesus** (so we could ask him a few well-prepared questions)
> **Dolly Parton** (to sing)
> **Rex Harrison/Terry Thomas** (can't

decide which one would get on best
with Stephen Fry)

The trick is to think unique and be original. From yet another vault at mysinglefriend.com we've dug out these winning profiles. Some may seem off-the-wall, but believe us, they've worked. Why? Because they stand out…

The Short but Sweet

'She is a bit away with the fairies, but in a good way.'

The Animal

'If Greg were an animal he would be a dog. Bow-legged, barrel-chested and walks with a swagger in his tail… dependable, lovable and house-trained. A Crufts winner. Greg is as adaptable as they come. The professional boyfriend. Needs a girl to keep him on his toes and to help him stock his fridge.'

The A to Z Profile

'A is for always there when you need her
B is for beautiful
C is for caring
D is for dependable
E is for her bra size and they are fabulous

I'd better stop there or she may kill me, but you get the gist. She is some hot tottie and deserves to meet some of the classier men the world has to offer – she is a diamond trapped in the rough and needs someone to help her sparkle.'

The Good Egg Profile

'When I made him see *Pride and Prejudice* with me he sympathized when I jumped at Mr Darcy slamming a door (although I think this was because he'd stolen my free Penguin). He's funny and kind and he has a full compost bin. He's not an expert cook, but he's trying very hard to become at least passable. He now knows the difference between boil and simmer. Well done! When I've just been dumped he takes me to the pub and sometimes disco dancing as well. Even on a school night.'

The 'Slightly Dippy' Profile

'She is a liability. She'll have you looking for her handbag, her keys, her mobile phone (she is on her 15th phone in four years) and her dignity. Raised by magpies, she is a petty thief and has been on the run since holding up a West Cornwall Pasty Co. I cannot cope with her criminal ways any longer. Please remove her from my life. Thank you.'

The Topical Profile

'A great bloke. Only this morning he asked me what phone I was using. I said, "A Motorola Timeport." He replied, "That's saaaaad, you need to upgraaade," so I said, "Well you need to upgrade... to a new face!" He nearly soiled himself. He said he had Kenco coming out of his nostrils, which made me laugh... The best phrase to sum Tim up would be Evolution Not Revolution, which is good, as he evolves, he doesn't ... revolve...?'

Remember, if you really can't think of anything this good then don't shy away from doing it altogether. Just do your best and you're bound to stand out...

What Next?

So, your profile is online, your description is hopefully sharp, relevant and interesting (maybe even witty), your photo uplifting and happy. You sit and wait. Nothing happens.

Don't panic! Before you consider taking your own life or getting another kitten, we have some good, road-tested advice for you.

Get Emailing

Whether you like it or not, you simply have to get in there and send emails. Old-fashioned (normal) etiquette (where a girl waits for a guy to make a move) doesn't exist on the internet. So say hello to the people you like the look of. Talk to as many people as possible. Not everyone will respond, but keep active and you'll get replies sooner or later. Most sites have a 'new members' section. As you're a newbie, too, why not start talking to them? They won't be setting up several dates with other members, so you can get in there first. Bingo.

Play Favourites

Most sites have 'favourites' – add as many people as you can. We like the analogy that a site is like a pop concert – how is someone meant to find you? By putting them in your favourites you are ensuring that you are both in the bar at the same time. Don't be too picky when it comes to favourites, either; remember, we don't all look like our picture, so you could be pleasantly surprised after chatting and maybe sharing more pictures.

Expand Your Criteria

There will be a 'criteria' section that you fill in when you join your online dating agency, and that you can subsequently change. If you expand your area and age criteria you'll pick up more new members and get more options. We have far-flung couples getting together all the time... so you never know.

Freshen Up...

On mysinglefriend.com, every time you log in you move to the top of the searches. That's important to keep you noticed. If you're on another site, find out what gets you noticed. Ask your agency what will keep your profile at the top of the searches.

Changing your picture now and then will refresh your pro-file, and think about updating your words every so often, too. For example, if you mentioned Christmas in your profile and summer's coming up, that's not going to look good, is it?

Lastly, Our Online Dating Do's and Don'ts

✓ **Do** make your online profile stand out – a funny profile works best every time.

✓ **Do** use an honest and *useful* picture in your profile (a clear and close-up shot of your smiley face will work better than a photo of you windsurfing back in '89!).

✓ **Do** be proactive and use all of the site's key features and benefits (for example, ask their customer services team for tips, though you won't necessarily get a response from some sites). Get the most for your money.

✗ **Don't** wait for someone else to make a move. It's the 21st century – get in there!

✗ **Don't** feel snubbed if someone doesn't bite. There are plenty more fish.

✗ **Don't** be dishonest – you'll waste your own time and get found out anyway.

Meeting Your Online Date

✓ **Do** always let someone know who, when and where you are meeting, and let them know when you are on your way home too.

✓ **Do** always meet in a public place with people around you.

✓ **Do** go with your instincts. If you feel uncomfortable, make a polite exit. If you are having a whale of a time, squeeze in a cheeky kiss so they know you want to see them again.

✗ **Don't** ever meet at your house or workplace – keep your personal information personal, and take your own safety seriously.

✗ **Don't** meet at the restaurant or bar you are planning to go visit. Instead, meet five minutes down the road, and take that time to walk and talk (and get rid of the small talk) so you both arrive at your venue feeling a bit more relaxed.

✗ **Don't** rush into love (or bed) – remember: your new crush is *still* virtually a stranger.

And most importantly...

✓ **Do** have fun!

Chapter Five

'Really? I Collect Gravel, Too'

knowing what you want and what people want from you

What do you want from your partner? Well, you want someone you can slob out on the sofa with. You want someone who will rub your tired feet after you've missed the bus and had to walk home in the rain. You want someone who will bring you a cup of tea without you asking for it – and it won't have any horrid bits floating in it.

Trouble is, you've got to meet this person first. And how on earth can you spot the right one for you? *Is* there a right person for everyone? Hearing a loved-up couple say things like,

'When we first clapped eyes on each other, we just knew,' you might be forgiven for thinking that...

- There's one person on the planet for everyone (and you can't find yours).
- It'll *never* happen to you.
- You feel nauseous all of a sudden.

Truth is – that loved-up couple from before? They didn't really 'know'. They just hoped. The fact is, there are thousands of people you could date within a 10-mile radius of where you sit right now (okay, not you, person sitting in a remote cottage in the Scottish Highlands), but you won't get to meet them all. So it ends up being the people we meet that we fall for.

Yes, that means if you don't meet new people, you won't find a partner. And you only need one at a time. It's time to meet some newbies.

What You Want from a Partner

The trick of dating is to manage your expectations, so have a think about the things you'd want from a partner. Make a list if you want. Things like this...

- **Social status** Is it important to you? There are still some people who consider class very important, and even if you are not one of them it's worth remembering that we're still very conscious of social status in this country.

- **Job** Do you work very unsociable hours and therefore need to meet someone who either works similar hours or at least is able to deal with it?

- **Films/music/books** How important is cultural stuff to you? And would it matter if your date wasn't bothered? Same with sport.

- **Nights out** What's your idea of a good time? If you spent your youth in fields off the M25, the chances are you're not going to hit it off with a teetotaller who thinks clubs are where you go to play chess. But then again, who knows? Which leads us on to...

- **Drinking/smoking/drugs** Will you be bothered if your partner is a smoker and you're not? If you *hate* smoking don't get into a relationship with a smoker thinking you will change them. You won't. All you will do is create an atmosphere of resentment in the relationship.

- **Food** Veggie? Or committed carnivore? Another tricky area. Carnivores like nothing better than getting a veggie to lapse. Most veggies feel the smell of a meaty Sunday roast (or poached haddock) might just make them leave home.

- **Children** If you are not prepared to accept existing children as part of the package, then don't go there – you cannot ever compete and nor should you try. It's worth bearing in mind that there are upsides to stepchildren, though, so don't rule someone out for having children already. They could end up being great friends and will almost certainly make someone a kinder, softer human being.

- **No way, José** You need to think about what makes someone a total non-starter. What are the things you simply have to have from your date, or won't put up with from them? Do you have any religious or political considerations? It's very, very early to start thinking about marriage and kids, but if your potential date tells you they're never, ever having children and you very much want them, it may not be worth bothering. Bear in mind though that you will rarely get someone (especially a man) to make loud declarations of wanting to hear the pitter-patter of tiny feet so don't take anti-children claims too seriously unless they have had themselves 'done'.

    Too often, people start relationships thinking things will sort themselves out further down the line. They rarely do.

- **But I want a tall man...** Then you are being too picky. It's common that a girl won't date a guy less than six feet tall (we blame the resurgence of the stiletto) but this is really restricting your fun – and your chance to date. If you think of all the famously humorous men throughout history, the lead singer you'd give your left arm to snog and the gorgeous movie star you'd kill to meet – half of them are going to be too short for you. Yet now you want to discount half of them? Stop limiting your chances.

- **But I want a stick-thin girl...** Then you are being too picky. It's common for a guy to say 'no fat girls' when what he actually means is that he doesn't want an unhealthy or obese girlfriend. Most girls have some fat on them, and most girls – athletic or curvy – *think* they're fat anyway. If a girl says she is curvaceous, she may well be slender. Give it a chance, as the photo may not really be one you can judge realistically. If you're a girl and you're worried about not being thin enough, trust us – men would rather date someone with curves than a skinny girl.

- **He/she is too old for me...** Here you go again. If you think of all your icons, the lead singers, the movie stars, etc, etc... half of them are going to be too old for you. Stop limiting your chances. Women seem to have more sense and not mind if her other half has a few years on her, but men, a quick word. On mysinglefriend.com we often see a male profile where the 'gentleman' is 42 but wanting to date a girl between the ages of 28 and 32. Please stop this, would you? Women can still have babies at 42 you know, and you are in essence preventing yourself from meeting the likes of Jennifer Aniston, Demi Moore and Sharon Stone. Madness.

Meanwhile, we notice at mysinglefriend.com that the younger guy will leave options open for an older woman. We hope this is because the younger generation have more sense (*over* the Mrs Robinson syndrome!), and that they won't in turn revert to only wanting 'younger models'.

Here are some good reasons why an older woman is a great choice:

- She knows more about 'the bedroom'.
- She invests in beautifully made matching underwear (no white knickers here).
- She has seen more stuff (she knows more about the world and is likely to be more open-minded).
- She knows herself (she won't be puking into the loo by midnight, and flying off the handle at the smallest thing).
- You know what you are going to get. By their mid-30s, women have found their feet in terms of style, body image and opinions.
- She can drive you to college.

Any truth in the rumour opposites attract? Who makes this stuff up? We aren't *attracted* to one another because we like or hate the same movies – that's called 'having things in common'. What we're attracted to is…

In the first 10 minutes… someone physically attractive.

In the first half an hour… someone physically attractive who is easy to talk to.

By week two… someone physically attractive who has slept with you.

In year one… someone physically attractive who sleeps with you regularly and whose personality traits sustain your interest.

In year two… someone whose personality traits sustain your interest, and whom you don't find physically nauseating.

And so on…

Then, of course, there is the 'creep up on you' crush, when you first of all find someone interesting, then fascinating, then gorgeous. This usually ends in a best-friend couple. Aww.

'Things in common' is for sparking conversation. This is because it is easier to listen to someone when they are sharing something you know about, care about or want to learn about. It's not to be mistaken for attraction, though.

If you find yourself drawn to one another whenever you meet, then you've got a spark. But it's rather tough to gauge a friendly spark from a sexy spark. On the upside, very few men or women will be able to keep the sexy spark a secret for long.

What Your Partner Wants

How on earth can you know what your partner wants? Easy-peasy. They want perfection. But what is the perfect catch? Well, it could be you, if...

- **You look the business** People are simple, rather shallow creatures. They like shiny things. They also like to be seen with a partner who looks like they take pride in themselves. No, you don't need to look like Beyoncé or Brad; just that you respect your partner enough to make an effort for them.

- **You show love** Love is the fuel on which we all run. Don't be stingy with yours.

- **You're independent** There's nothing less attractive than someone who needs constant attention, night and day; who is always on the phone; who is always unhappy for one reason or another (too hot, too cold, tired, hungry, full); who *whines* all the time. People hate having to give accounts of their movements and will scarper sharpish if you start demanding to know where they've been all day, with whom, and whether or not they were attractive.

  If you do this because your last partner cheated on you, then you're making your new lover pay for your ex's misdemeanours, which isn't fair. And, frankly, you run a much higher risk of having another partner cheat on you.

  So be emotionally independent, have a good time without your partner and understand that they need to have a good time without you.

- **You show respect** You don't criticize, demean or belittle your partner, and never, ever in public. You listen to your partner's opinions, even if you don't agree with them. You don't try and change your partner. If you're a vegetarian and they're not, you don't constantly nag them about giving up meat. If they like their hair long and you like it short, you don't go on and on about getting it cut. Why? Because your partner is a real, live human being, not just an extension of you, and you should respect them and their individuality.

- **You know that men and women are different** Social attitudes to this have changed comparatively recently and it's now considered acceptable to admit that – yes – men and women are different and want different things, and that they have different skills, strengths and weaknesses.

- **You don't nag** Well, not about the little stuff anyway. Ladies, take the Lavatory Seat Test. Do you moan when he leaves it up? Yes? Well, here's the thing. If him leaving the seat up is part of a larger package of things you despise about him, well, then you clearly need to think long and hard about the relationship. If he's a great guy and he loves you, makes you feel good about yourself, buys you nice presents on your birthday *but* leaves the toilet seat up, why not let it slide?

- **You understand they've got friends and family** We have a tendency to think that our partner's world is defined by your relationship. It isn't. They have family and friends who were around a long time before you, and they're going to have commitments to those people, some of which may be unpopular with you or inconvenient for you. So if their best pal rings up in a state because she's just been dumped, then sorry, that meal you cooked may just have to go cold. If his brother has just gone bankrupt, then he may need to help out. Your understanding of these situations will make you a champion partner.

Spotting the Right Date for You

- **First impressions** Don't necessarily go on them. Ever noticed how people who are beautiful can become ugly, and someone you thought quite plain can become beautiful as you get to know them?

- **Laughter** Dating is all about having fun. Nobody's saying that you and your date should be stand-up comedians, but you need to be able to make each other laugh – having a laugh is what it's all about. Plus, there is a medical reason – endorphins are released when you laugh that makes you feel good.

- **Comfort** Use your instinct before you go on a date. How does this person make you feel when you're talking to them or emailing them? If there's a little voice in your head telling you something's not quite right then listen to it, because feeling comfortable with this person is of paramount importance, it really is. Your date must make you feel comfortable and happy about yourself and who you are.

- **Lust** You do need to fancy your date, of course you do, but that doesn't mean you have to be bowled over by their looks and dribbling with lust at the mere mention of their name. Give it time – lust can grow even if there is just the tiniest spark there.

- **Trial and error** Sorry, but practice makes perfect. You need to get out there and start dating so you can find out who's right for you. Just make sure you have fun doing it.

- **Expectations** Don't have stupid, unrealistic expectations. Nobody is going to arrive in a helicopter to take you for dinner. If they do they are almost certainly a drug lord and so probably not the most suitable person to be dating as far as your granny is concerned.

Chapter Six

'But I've Got All My Own Warts!'

the lowdown on who not to date

Right, you're pretty sure you know what type of person you want to meet. Now for the not-so-good news.

Like it or not, there are some real fruitcakes out there; people who (gasp) may not have read this book, or have read this book and thought that it didn't apply to them, perfect as they already are. The chancers, the cowboys, the big-heads, the rampant rotters and bunny-boilers. Yup, they're all coming soon to a dating venue near you.

Weeding out the wheat from the chaff is one of the most difficult aspects of dating. Because you seriously do not want to end up with one of this lot...

The Wedding Planners

Woah there. Slow down. Anyone who discloses their urgent desire for marriage or children on or before a first date is to be, if not actively avoided, approached as though meeting a famished tiger on the way back from the butchers – with infinite, immeasurable caution.

Why? Because this is not the kind of person to let nature take its course. They want control. They want a life of certainty and uniformity. They probably read the last pages of a novel first and will demand to know what Christmas present you have bought them, saying, 'It'll avoid embarrassment if you tell me now.'

It is really simple – you date, some people get married, some don't. Nobody should be expected to commit to anything in advance. They shouldn't be asking you to sign an 'in theory marriage is not out of the question' contract before buying you a gin and tonic. If they do and you carry on with the relationship, mark our words. Your life is about to be planned for you, right down to the tiniest detail.

The Age Gappers

Beware anyone who is clearly lying about their age, either by standing before you and barefacedly shaving a decade off their obvious wear and tear, or by employing any kind of device aimed at making them look younger. Men who use that strange blue/black hair dye, for example; women in their 40s wearing midriff-revealing tops and ankle chains; someone whose children call them by their Christian name.

The fact is that well-adjusted people don't have hang-ups about their age, so don't bother lying about it or trying to cover it up. Anyway politeness says you shouldn't ask.

The Other Halves

You know, the ones who say...

'I've got a boyfriend/girlfriend but it's nothing serious. I mean, really, you'd hardly even say we were together.'

Which translates as: 'I've got a boyfriend/girlfriend who doesn't know that I'm a lying, cheating backstabbing vulture.'

'I've got a boyfriend/girlfriend but we're on the verge of splitting up.'

Which translates as: 'Yeah, when my boyfriend/girlfriend finds out that I've got an old, waxy candle where my heart should be, and snake venom for blood.'

Which translates as: 'Not that he/she is aware of this funky new rule I've just this second introduced into our relationship.'

If you can easily steal someone from another relationship then they can just as easily be stolen from you, so prepare for a rocky road. For your own sanity, tell your potential beau to chuck out their dirty laundry and buy new sets before embarking on a trip down love lane with you. Somebody with a partner – whatever the stage of that relationship – is not someone to date. You are wasting your own time, not theirs.

The Generation Exes

Are they always taking about exes? Are they? Be careful of anyone who yaks on about previous relationships or, even worse, talks incessantly about *one specific relationship* – it means you're the rebound shag. They will tell you that they're over their ex, and maybe you'll want to believe them, but let's face it: people who are over their exes do not discuss them with strangers at parties. They're not over their ex. They just want something squishy to do to help them forget. If it's okay with you that they are aiming low to massage their egos then fine, but face facts, enjoy it for what it is (it almost certainly won't last) and go in with your eyes open. Heck, maybe the ego boost is what you need, too.

The Boss

Having a relationship with someone at work is okay, as long as you're careful. However, a relationship with your *boss* is a dangerous one and should probably be avoided. Yes, there's a so-wrong-it's-right exotica about it in the early stages, but come on – you're putting grief and heartache in the post. Sooner or later it *will* arrive.

The Best Mate's Brother or Sister

Yes, there's a so-wrong-it's-right exotica about it in the early stages, but come on – you're putting grief and heartache in the post. Sooner or later it *will* arrive. Though just occasionally Cupid might be doing his thing.

Your Neighbour

Yes, there's a so-wrong-it's-right exotica etc., etc., etc...

The Parent Trappers

No, not parents themselves but people who seem overly obsessed with their own dear ma and pa. Don't get us wrong – we love our parents. We love other people's parents, too. But we've spread our wings, left the nest, moved on literally and figuratively. And this is a healthy, normal, well-adjusted thing to do. Could it be that someone who spends lots of time with their parents, or who talks about them all the time or parrots their opinions might be a) *not* all that well-adjusted and/or b) impossible to shoehorn away from their family, meaning you will have to face up to a future of their mum and dad smiling at you over breakfast, from the back seat of your car, from your sofa, on your honeymoon...

Bad Boys and Vixens

So easy to spot, and even easier to fall for. That's because they're professional seducers. They ruthlessly tease their victims into submission then let you dangle, besotted, hoping that despite all the available evidence to the contrary you are going to be the one to tame this bad person.

We've all dated one and we all come back for more. Why do they seem so alluring? Because they are. The bastards.

The bad boys and vixens can be spotted quite early on in a dating scenario. They will almost certainly be late for dates, not bother with excuses and not listen to you when you pipe up that you've been sitting waiting for them for half an hour. The BB or V is a narcissist, no doubt with 'childhood issues', and when you (eventually) wake up after investing your time comforting, supporting and excusing them, you'll realize that you can't change them, and worse, may have lost precious self-esteem.

Get rid early doors is our advice, as they'll almost certainly break your heart. Trouble is, it takes real backbone to chuck one as they are so bloody attractive. Bastards.

The Commitment-phobes

Difficult to spot from the outset as the commitment-phobe may well start the new relationship with gusto. However, it doesn't take long for them to 'feel trapped', and consequently make *you* feel as if you are smothering them. Whether the CP is looking for absolute perfection (and is therefore easily disappointed) or just loves the buzz of a new relationship is immaterial. Don't waste precious moments of your life trying to find out – they just don't want to commit to you. If you think you've got yourself a CP, ask the questions, get your answers then get out and let them bugger up someone else's month.

IT Boys

As in, people who work with computers. We should start by saying that contrary to this old-fashioned pigeonhole (and sorry, but it is mainly guys who work in IT) not *all* geeks should be avoided. He can fix your computer; he can fix your friends' computers and is capable of using all the household gadgets you can't. He earns a decent living, he has good logic and he won't cheat on you (place him in a room with the sexiest woman you know *and* the latest dual-core Pentium something or other and you'll see this in action).

The geek is here to stay. He used to be a hardcore computer programmer – but now the geek can work in 'meejah' and be super cool.

Some geeks should be avoided though – and that's the geek who can't speak human. You'll know who he is as soon as he opens his mouth. His first language was binary, he calls his car 'she' and (if you ever make it to his bedroom) has oriental calligraphy on his duvet cover.

If you do really like someone and they are displaying signs of rampant nuttiness, don't back off and hope for the best – most nutty tendencies come with insecurity. Be nicer to them, make sure they know you are a sure thing and they should mellow out – if they don't then you might have to spell it out to them.

One final word on the nutters. Remember that everyone has their own little 'thing' that winds them up. It's up to you to decide what you can live with and what you can't. Half the fun is finding out...

'Nobody Loves Me, Everybody Hates Me, Think I'll Go and Eat Worms...'

beating the bad-image blues

Let's face it: you're here because your last relationship went belly-up. It wasn't working out so you gave your partner their marching orders, or – ugh – you were given yours. And even though being single and in the dating game should theoretically be an exciting time, full of fun and endless adventure and possibility, you're feeling bruised, battered and about as attractive as a wet flannel hanging off a doorknob. Worse still, you simply can't get the spectre of your last relationship out of your head.

The bad news is that needy victim is not a good look. Erotically speaking, it's down there with picking your toenails and curry farts. The *good* news is that there is something you can do about it and, as ever, if you've got a problem, we have the answers. So, fire away...

1. 'I'm Still Stuck on My Ex!'

Being dumped is the equivalent of somebody kidnapping your self-esteem then sending it back to you, piece by piece. And for a long time after the split you'll be walking around feeling like you've got a boot-print on your face and 'Loser' tattooed across your forehead. The emotions? A real pick 'n' mix of all the nasty ones: worthlessness, hurt, powerlessness, resentment, anger, frustration, a bit more anger and – yes – just a *soupçon* more hurt on the side.

Saying you should 'get over it' is like saying you should learn Mandarin – easier said than done; Mandarin has loads of different dialects, for one thing. And, more to the point,

How the hell do you expect me to get over my ex when my heart is in pieces, my bed is lined with soggy Kleenex, I didn't dare leave the flat last week just in case my ex had lost my mobile number and wanted to call me at home, and the last time I went to the corner shop a homeless person gave me 50p for a cup of tea?

Well, nobody ever said it would be easy.

- **Let go of your ex** Yes, and nobody said that would be easy either, but look – if you're waiting in for their call then you're still harbouring thoughts of a reconciliation, and that's not a good idea. True, couples do get back together when one has left the other, and there are obviously success stories. But they're rare. When one partner walks out the relationship gets like a supermarket trolley with wobbly wheels. You can try steering that trolley all you want. You can tell yourself that it's fine because you simply can't be arsed to return to the entrance and get yourself a new trolley, and besides, it's already got loads of shopping in it, but it's not – it's not fine. And before you know it, volunteers will be pulling it out of a river with bits of algae hanging off it.

  And you don't want that, do you? You don't want a dirty, smelly old trolley with a wobbly wheel, a bit of baby sick on the seat and somebody's money-off vouchers in the bottom of it. You want a nice, shiny, new trolley.

Better still, you want a shag. So look forwards, not back, and…

- **Learn from the experience** Why did you get dumped? It may be too late now, but perhaps you can learn enough from the break-up to be a better (or at least more informed) partner next time. So, was it because…

  You just didn't make enough effort with your partner. Had you got complacent? Were you taking them for granted? If so, why? They walked out, but maybe your behaviour was subconsciously saying that you wanted to get shot of them. Of course, you could just be the type of person who takes people for granted, in which case, um… You might want to work on that particular character flaw.

  You weren't good enough friends. The most successful relationships are two best mates who sleep together. You might have got the latter part right but what about the friends bit? The right person for you will be someone who can bring both into your life.

  You wanted different things. Ouch. Just about the toughest break-up due west of infidelity with a member of your family is the old 'we wanted different things'. Whether it's marriage, babies, lifestyle – whatever – if neither of you is prepared to compromise then something's got to give. Either that or you've got yourself another faulty trolley. The thing to bear in mind about this kind of break-up is that you can't assume someone's going to change just because you get into a serious relationship with them. Some differences just won't be papered over.

You were friends, not lovers. If you weren't sharing bedroom antics there was clearly a problem on both sides. Maybe you didn't realize it but your eyes were wandering, too. Either way, you're both well out of it, but hopefully you can remain friends.

• **Move on...** How will you know when you're finally free of your ex? Well...

Did a day go by when you didn't think about them? Did it?

When you do think of them, are the feelings you get (of anger, hatred, mourning) less intense than they used to be?

Have you stopped talking about them non-stop to anyone who will listen, including the poor kid who delivers your free newspaper on a Wednesday afternoon?

Have you stopped fantasizing about either a) getting back together or b) the squishing sound they will make as you run them over in your car?

If you can answer 'Yes' to two of those questions and a 'Kind of' to at least one other then it's time to get back on the horse.

- **Oh, it was you doing the chucking?** Don't get the hump. Nobody's saying it wasn't hard for you, either. Of course it was – it was a big step; it took guts. But, hey, you did the dumping. You'll get over it a damn sight more quickly than the poor sod you've just binned.

2. 'I Lack Self-esteem!'

It's not true that you need to first love yourself in order for someone else to love you; there are heaps of self-loathing people in relationships. The trouble is, those relationships are usually unhealthy and characterized by one partner hating the other for being stupid enough to love them or, even more catastrophically, by emotional and physical abuse. So no, you don't *need* self-esteem to get on in the dating game, but for all parties involved, it really, really helps.

How, though? The first thing to do is to take stock. Ask yourself the following questions and think about the answers. How much of this stuff was dictated not by you but by your ex-partner, or the simple mechanics of day-to-day life as a couple?

What films do you like?

Same with music?

What skills or interests have you let go?

What are the things your partner used to do that you can do for yourself?

What do you like to wear?

Which friends have you neglected?

Where do you like to go out at night?

What kind of television programmes do you like to watch?

Can you cook?

Where do you like to eat out?

And so on. The idea is to recover the person you really are, not the person you have become. Look at your interests and desires and start making your day-to-day decisions based on what *you* want, rather than what someone else wanted or what was convenient for the relationship. Next, go further and start to actively pursue those pastimes you let slide. Is there a friend your ex-partner disapproved of? Then get them back in your life. Did your ex loathe modern art? Take a trip to the Tate Modern and take your mate – ha! Not only will you win yourself back, but you will also start to realize that you don't actually *need* a significant other in your life. There's nothing less attractive than a needy person anyway, and you will be taking the first important steps to a fun and fabulous dating life.

3. 'I Can't Talk to Strangers!'

We beg to differ. You can. It's called small talk and anybody can do it. Even you. In fact, *especially* you.

But, like anything else, it takes a bit of effort and practice. Start by making the odd bit of small talk with people you meet in day-to-day life: shopkeepers, a passenger on the bus, a person in front of you in a queue. Smile, say something utterly casual and throwaway, like, 'At least it's stopped chucking it down,' and leave it there.

Try it, go on. Bet you they don't bite. Bet you they don't turn round and tell you to eff off. The truth is, that bit of small talk will have helped to make their day more pleasant.

Next, you need to put yourself in a position where you

have to talk to strangers, but on your terms. So, why not...

- **Take a class** Those interests that you re-ignited – go a step further and take an evening class. You'll meet new faces, and not because you're trying to get in each other's pants but because you're interested in the same thing.

- **Join a club** It can be anything: hang-gliding, chess, creative writing, sailing – whatever floats your boat (ha ha). Either way, it's the same principle as above.

- **Go online** If you feel too nervous to relate to real, live people, join an internet forum or message board devoted to a subject you like. There you'll have hundreds of people all with the same interest and you can get chatting – with zero pressure. More often than not the forum will organize get-togethers and you'll have the chance to meet these people in the flesh.

- **Volunteer** Hey, you could be one of those people who fishes broken trolleys out of the river at the weekend...

But what if you've put yourself out there and you still get tongue-tied? There's plenty of communication ammo later on in the book, but for now here are a few basic pointers.

- **Ask lots of questions** People *love* answering them.

- **Be a good listener** Don't just use their bit of the conversation to plan your next witticism, but listen to what they say and let it inform your chat.

- **Say something pleasant** Not necessarily a compliment as such, just, 'How nice to see a smile,' or, 'Blimey, you know lots about shopping trolleys...'

- **Who dares wins** Start a conversation, ask a few questions, give out a few compliments – you might even enjoy it.

- **Smile and laugh** But don't overdo it or they'll think you're taking the piss.

- **Never boast** Too often people jump in with some inappropriately self-aggrandizing statement. Although we would never, ever do that because we're great.

- **Take the knock-backs** You make a joke and nobody laughs. You're saying something and are rudely interrupted. You make a remark that is ignored. Your suggestion seems to go unheard but is then made by somebody else and taken up. Shit happens. It happens to us all. Inwardly seethe, then move on.

4. 'I Lack Self-confidence!'

Then it's time to start liking what you see in the bathroom mirror. If you've got this far then you should already be halfway there, but bear these points in mind to keep the positive you firing on all cylinders and that negative, nasty person who occasionally lives in your head quiet.

- **Try to look your best** It's easy to fall into the letting-yourself-go trap when you're feeling like the world's passing you by on its way to somewhere really cool and interesting. So don't let yourself go. Thinking that you've got 'nobody to look good for' is one of the symptoms of your confidence famine. Plan your wardrobe and stay fresh, fragrant and fabulous at all times. It's good for your self-esteem, plus you never know when you might bump into the love of your life.

- **The voice in your head that tells you that you can't. Tell it to shut the hell up** Nobody wants a resident critic telling them what a failure they are, so give that voice the boot. Thinking positive is a major step to feeling it, too.

- **Switch the lights on** If you were in a room that was too dark, you wouldn't sit there wishing it was less dark, would you? No. You'd stand up, walk over to the light switch and turn on the lights. In other words, you'd do something about it. Next time you feel like nothing's working out, ask yourself what you can do to change the situation. No, of course the answer won't be as easy as going to the light switch – but by deciding to do something about it you'll already be part-way to banishing those moody blues.

- **Don't beat yourself up** When you're down, it's too easy to dwell on all those mistakes you've made and the opportunities you've missed – it's that voice again. But imagine you were talking to a friend. What would they say? They'd probably say, 'Don't worry about it.' They'd say, 'Laugh, grimace, wince, make a pistol with your fingers and put it to your head, and then... move on.'

- **Treat yourself** There's a reason this bit of advice is the world's biggest cliché. It's because it's true. You are your own best friend, and it's time to show your friend how much you like having them around. Buy them stuff. Pamper them. Tell them how great they look.

- **Stop blaming your ex for your predicament** Yes, maybe they are to blame, but trust us – they don't give a shit either way. Decide it was partly your choice or fault – learn from it and move on.

'I Hate My Body!'

You're not alone. Everybody has something about themselves they despise. Whether we like it or not, we all buy into the media image of what constitutes a perfect body which, let's be honest, we all know is airbrush-tastic anyway. Building your self-esteem and confidence is a massive start in conquering body paranoia, but we wouldn't be doing our job if we didn't have a few more tips to help you on your way.

- **Don't slag off your body** Sad fact of life, but we cope with criticism better than we do with compliments. So much so that when we're given a compliment we can't help but turn it into a criticism. Trouble is, this kind of self-criticism comes from within. We're too keen to draw attention to the worst bits of our bodies, saying, 'Ugh, I feel fat today,' or 'My hair looks like poo,' so we're training ourselves and other people to focus on the bad bits. So stop it.

- **Don't avoid the full-length mirror** Everybody stares at their face in the mirror. A lot. Whether you're doing your make-up or shaving, you're spending a lot of time looking at your boat race. Ah, but what about the full-length? Once a week? Once a month? Only on very special occasions? We thought so. Here's a new rule: check yourself out every day, full-length and preferably naked. You need to get comfy with your body. If you're thinking, 'But I won't like what I see,' well, that's the problem and that's why you've got to do it. You're not facing your fear. So, get your kit off, get in front of the full-length and face up to all those imperfections. Try it, go on. See? They're not that bad, are they?

- **Remember that sexiness comes from inside** And Marilyn Monroe was a size 16, so...

- **Say bollocks to 'perfection'** The fashion and make-up industries earn vast amounts of dosh by making you feel bad about your body. The worse they can make you feel about your looks, the more money they will earn. Nobody's saying you should boycott their products – just their ethics. So, instead of trying to match up to whichever flavour-of-the-month clothes-horse is staring at you from a billboard, give yourself the more realistic goal of feeling comfortable with your own looks.

- **Ask yourself if your date will care** Because the answer, dear reader, is no.

A lack of self-esteem and self-confidence and a bruised and battered heart is not something you're going to get over just by glancing at a chapter in a book – we know that. But please bear some of the above in mind. Doing so will at least help you to be a happier, more fun person to be around. And a better date to boot.

Chapter Eight

'You Talkin' to Me?'

how to be good at talking, listening and the other stuff in between

When we're nervous, our heart rate rises, we begin to perspire and the 'fight or flight' mechanism kicks in, which means we get the urge either to go home where the milk and cookies are, or to grossly exaggerate our own character beyond recognition.

What else? Oh yes, your mouth goes dry, you clam up, your mind goes blank. 'What's your name?' your date asks you. 'Yes, and the forecast was rain,' you reply. Oh dear. And the thing is, you're a high-flyer. You make your living influencing, negotiating, making an impact, dealing with conflict and managing difficult people every day. But, somehow, when it comes to dating, everything seems that little bit more tricky. Calm down, dear. What you need is a good talking to...

Talking Sense
(and other good communication tips)

Find Common Ground Quick

In Chapter 2 we talked about sidling up to someone at a party and asking how they know the host. That particular tip was brought to you by the Find Common Ground Department of this book, which also suggests talking through other possible shared interests, such as where you're spending Christmas or going on your holidays. It's worth pointing out that if someone doesn't try and meet your conversation, then you might as well give up – they're either socially inadequate or they hate you. The Find Common Ground Department thanks you for your time and wishes you a safe journey home.

Talk about Current Events

Probably safer to stick with Jordan's boob jobs rather than the socio-political situation in Jordan, but you know the kind of thing we mean.

Remember You're Not a Product

Nobody likes to listen to some stranger list their attributes and qualities so don't drone on and on about how great you are. Remember those kids at school who were always prefects? You'll sound like one of them. Still, you do have to big yourself up a bit – just do it subtly, okay?

Don't Be Too Self-deprecating

Everybody who's seen a Hugh Grant movie thinks a sure-fire way to charm the birds off the trees is to talk themselves down – in a slightly hesitant, bumbling way. It works for Hugh Grant because he's devastatingly attractive. Unless you are also devastatingly attractive you shouldn't be pointing out your own flaws. Plenty of time for them to find out what a toad you are later, so…

Be 'Up' and Confident

Yes! Really! Which means smiling a lot and being optimistic. Not too optimistic, but if 'Hey, this dip tastes great! It's the best dip I've ever had!' is at one end of the scale, and, 'I really, really hope the roof doesn't cave in and kill us all,' is at the other, you want to be about halfway between the two.

Don't Tell Jokes

Okay, a little gag is good. The odd one-liner. But please, please don't start any conversation with, 'Two gay blokes walk into a bar, right...' or whatever other gem you heard at work that afternoon.

Ask Lots of Questions

About their work, family, interests and so on. Don't fire questions like Jeremy Paxman on angel dust (and whatever you do, listen to the answers), but do ask them. Questions show interest, and whether or not they're reciprocated can also be a good indicator of how the person feels about you. Put it this way: if they're not interested in you, they're not interested in you.

Pay Compliments

Generally speaking, people are crap at both giving and taking compliments. So, you'll have to work hard to make your compliments sound sincere – and not like you've just read a book on how to talk to people at parties. How do you do this? Well, as you've been listening to the advice of our Find Common Ground Department, you should by now have established a shared interest. So, keep your praise within your sphere of knowledge – that way you won't sound insincere. As for taking a compliment, say thank you. Whatever you do, don't belittle the compliment. There's absolutely nothing worse for the person giving it – they'll wish they'd stayed at home with milk and cookies, or spent the evening hiding under their duvet.

The Lost Art of Listening

Woah, rewind. What was all that stuff a few sentences back about *listening*? Yes, listening is where it's at.

'The most basic and powerful way to connect to another person is to listen,' says the American professor Rachel Naomi Remen. 'Just listen. Perhaps the most important thing we ever give each other is our attention. A loving silence often has far more power to heal and to connect than the most well-intentioned words.'

And how right she is. Listening involves hearing, understanding and judging – skills you have already, as you know how to breathe. But here are some additional tips for the early dating scene scenario.

Pay Attention

Look at the person talking to you. This sounds elementary – words like 'grandma' and 'suck eggs' are no doubt springing to mind. However, if you are on a first date, verbose French menu in hand, it can prove difficult. You may be distracted by your shoes pinching (hot tip: never wear new shoes on a date) or your dinner companion's 'unusual' shirt. You are taking a lot in – you can't help it; you are judging the person and the scenario. You are evaluating your date and trying to work out if you like them, and if they like you. You are also aware that every person in the room knows you are on a date. Yes, they *all know*; they are all laughing at you; their only topic of conversation is about you; there is spinach between your teeth and your skirt/shirt is tucked in so we can see your pants. Calm down and pay attention to the person who has made the effort to come and meet you. They feel the same way.

Don't Interrupt

It's easy to interrupt when you think you know what someone is going to say next, and we are all guilty of 'butting in' – that's usually okay with your friends as you know each other well, and probably do know what is about to be said and want to share something relevant. When you interrupt someone you don't know, however, it looks like you aren't listening, or aren't interested in hearing any further.

Understand

You can't really understand what someone is saying if you're busy thinking about what to say next. If you aren't sure you understand what they're talking about, just ask – your question will show that you are interested, not that you have only one operational brain cell. In a business meeting you might make a quick note (while trying to keep eye contact) of what to add to the conversation. On a date you don't have that luxury, so go with the flow.

Feedback

Do something to show you are listening – smile, frown, giggle, be silent, nod. You listen with your eyes as well as your ears, so delving into a handbag looking for lip-salve looks like you're thinking about something else, even if you happen to be listening. To sit your chin on top of a hand (or both hands) while engaging in eye contact (to dispel a myth – elbows on the table are fine if you aren't eating) is all encompassing. Your date will think you are interested.

A Promise...

If your date thinks you are interested in what they have to say, the chances are they'll like you. Even if they don't want to jump your bones, you will have made a good impression, networked, found a new restaurant or had a confidence boost… maybe even made a new friend.

Body-language Bollocks

In this next section we're going to be looking at what people who make a living out of that so-called science 'body language' say. These guys reckon it takes us between 90 seconds and four minutes to decide if we fancy someone, and that 55 per cent of our first impression comes from body language. Thirty-eight per cent is from the tone, speed and inflection of the voice and just seven per cent is from what the poor schmuck is actually saying. And according to those self-same 'experts', these are the things we should be looking out for.

Hair Fiddling

The one they talk about most often is the old 'playing with the hair' trick. If you haven't come across this before, welcome to the 21st century. If the person you're talking to is touching their hair, it is supposed to mean that they're interested – they think you're a fox. There's no science to the actual fiddle (how they do it will depend on their hairstyle) but it's worth remembering because it's meant to be, and indeed will be read by some people as, a subconscious act – what body language enthusiasts call a 'protean' signal.

Or maybe it just means... They've just bought some new conditioner, and it makes their hair feel really nice and soft. Because – come on – just because someone rakes a hand through their hair while they're talking to you doesn't necessarily mean they want to get it on, does it?

Eyebrow Raising

Did you see that eyebrow go up? Then assuming they're not trying to impersonate Groucho Marx, they're meant to be up for it. According to our old friends 'the experts', people all over the world are lifting their eyebrows when they see some-one they fancy. They can't help themselves, apparently. Like the old hair fiddle, it's a subconscious, protean signal. According to us? Well, since you ask...

Or maybe it just means... They've just had insane amounts of Botox syringed into their forehead and they're wondering why they've lost all sensation above their eyebrows.

Lip Parting

Watch their mouth. Did it open? Did it? Even just a tiny bit? It's another subconscious signal of sexual desire. Honest. The face is generally opening, you see: the mouth, the eyes – you may even find the nostrils flare. It's all about the face adopting an open, friendly expression. They might as well be hanging a sign off their nose saying, 'Wahay.'

> **Or maybe it just means...** Their mouth is opening because they're about to put some crisps into it. Or maybe their nostrils are flaring because that fragrance you're wearing is more oh, the toilet, than eau de toilette.

Clothes Fiddling

Sexually interested people start mucking about with their clobber. The 'experts' can't decide whether this is a displacement activity (i.e. you're all nervous and flustered so you start fiddling with things) or auto-erotic touching (i.e. you find this person so blimmin' sexy you simply can't wait to get your kit off).

> **Or maybe it just means...** Duh, it might just be that their jeans have gone up their bum. But still, if you're playing Doctor Body Language, that's a symptom to look out for.

Facial Touching

Are they stroking their own face? Running their hands across their chin, touching their mouth and ears? Then you're in. Once again the 'experts' argue about whether facial touching is merely displacement activity or full-on auto-erotic behaviour.

> **Or maybe it just means...** They're one of those shoe snobs we talked about earlier, and what's the quickest way to your feet?

Visual Voyaging – Come Again?

Well, 'visual voyaging' is what the 'experts' call it when somebody gives you a good looking-over. Us normal mortals call it being checked out. Fairly obvious that if somebody's checking you out then they're wondering what you look like in 99.9 per cent fewer clothes, but there you go – somebody got paid to call it 'visual voyaging'.

> **Or maybe it just means...** It's *you* with the zit that glows with the intensity of a sunburst. It's on your nose and they're trying desperately not to stare at it by looking anywhere else but at your nose.

Glass Rolling

The body tends to 'leak' its subconscious desires, so watch what the object of your affection is doing with their hands. Men, in particular, will play with something they're holding. No sniggering at the back there, we're being deadly serious. Guys will start to play with something circular – a glass, say – because it reminds them of a woman's breasts. Yes, really.

Or maybe it just means... Don't be ridiculous. They're thirsty, and it's your round.

Attention-seeking

Some people will go to extraordinary lengths to attract the attention of the opposite sex. Just look at Evel Knievel. But some would say to keep an eye out for more subtle devices. Again, those protean signals can mean that a person will subconsciously stand slightly apart from the crowd, which apparently is trying to make them appear unique and individual and thus catch your eye.

Or maybe it just means... They're the kind of self-obsessed, screeching attention-junkie that you'd do anything to avoid. Or they just don't happen to know anyone very well and have personal space issues.

Leaning in

Or 'perching' on the seat. If the body is moving forwards that's a good sign. They think you're gorgeous of the drop-dead variety.

Or maybe it just means... They're hard of hearing or the stool is too high.

Stealing Your Pen

And running off with it while shouting, 'Poo, poo, you smell...' As practised by school kids all over the world. Works a treat, too.

Or maybe it just means... They needed a new pen or wanted a fight.

Posture Paranoia

You may have noticed that we're slightly cynical of the whole body-language thing. And this extends to posture, too. Take the arms folded across the chest, for example. It's universally accepted that this is a defensive posture, so if your date was doing this you would be forgiven for wondering if they were sending out negative signals.

But what if they're just a bit chilly? Or they have a bit of cranberry sauce on their jumper? Actually, folding your arms across your chest is quite a self-comforting gesture – it's like hugging yourself – so it would be perfectly natural for your date to do this without it meaning they hate your guts. Let's take a look at some more posture stuff...

If the look is... **A brisk upright walk, oozing confidence from every pore.**

They might be saying... 'I'm bricking myself. Perhaps if I carry myself like this, everybody will think I'm really cool and confident. Let's give it a go...'

If the look is...
Hands on hips, assertively.

They might be saying... 'I went out running this morning, for an hour. So check out that stomach. Go on, look at it. Look, damn you.'

If the look is... **Sitting with legs crossed, foot kicking, seemingly bored.**

They might be saying... 'I'm just sitting, all right? Stop judging me.'

If the look is...
Hand to cheek, pensive.

They might be saying... 'Hmm, this new facial scrub really does the trick.'

If the look is... **Looking down, face turned away in what seems like disbelief.**

They might be saying... 'Oh, look, a doggy just came into the room. And he's wearing a cute little coat...' Or, 'Hmm, I like those slate tiles.'

If the look is... **Tilted head, showing extreme interest in your sparkling wit and repartee.**

They might be saying... 'I went swimming yesterday and forgot to take my goggles. I'm terrified of getting water in my eyes, so I swam with my head held above the water at an unnatural angle. I now have a crick in my neck that no amount of Deep Heat will shift and I can't wait to get away from this crashingly dull conversation and give it a massage in the bogs.'

If the look is... **Lifted eyebrow, obviously interested in what you have to say.**

They might be saying... 'I can't remember if I left the oven on or not.'

If the look is... **Feet pointing in your direction, the way the experts say denotes attraction.**

They might be saying... 'What am I? A

duck? My feet always point in this direction. I've told you before, stop judging me.'

If the look is... **Head resting in hand, eyes downcast, bored, perhaps?**

They might be saying... 'Yes, you're right, I'm bored.'

If the look is... **Clenching of fist, irritation you'd think.**

They might be saying... 'Oh no, it's time to get the bill.'

If the look is... **Cold sweat, pale face, dry mouth, trembling lip, visible high pulse, voice tremors, speech errors, varying speech tone. The classic symptoms of anxiety.**

They might be saying... 'I'm pissed.'

If the look is... **Blinking. According to the 'experts' this means they fancy you. But according to this 'expert' it means they're lying...**

They might be saying... 'See where all this body language stuff gets you?'

Which is our very, very long-winded way of saying that you have to take all of this body-language stuff with a pinch of salt.

Into the Bedroom and Beyond

The key to any relationship is communication – the lack of it is the main reason why relationships break down. But *too much* talking can be the kiss of death, especially when it comes to all that bedroom stuff. Sometimes it is more powerful to leave things unsaid. So how do you know how far to go?

Five Communication Commandments

1. The following questions do not necessarily need an honest answer.

   (i) Do these jeans make me look fat? Honestly, do they? I won't mind if you say they do...

   (ii) I thought Jane/John looked much better than me tonight. What did you think?

   (iii) Have you ever done that with anyone else?

   They just don't, okay?

2. Never begin any conversation with, **'What I need from this relationship is... a baby/a sports car/someone to stop my mother from hassling me.'** Yes, your needs are important, but try and be a bit more devious about getting them met.

3. Never, ever say, **'What are you thinking about now?'** Never say it, even if somebody holds a gun to your puppy dog's head and demands that you say it.

4. Oh, and while we're at it, try to steer clear of, **'You're very quiet. What's wrong?'** If you say this while 'supportively' stroking your partner's hair, they may well vomit on you. Or, worse, tell you that they're quiet because they're about to dump you for being cloying and needy, and that life with you is like being force-fed little spoonfuls of honey, one at a time.

5. Here's another one to avoid: **'If there was anything you didn't like about me, you would tell me, wouldn't you?'** As if. You may think you're being subtle and cunning, but your partner will see

through the ruse straight away. You're encouraging honesty for one reason only – so you can let rip on them about something that's been bugging the hell out of you. Look, you're not perfect (honestly, you're not), so you don't deserve perfection in return. Remember, there is always an advantage to every character trait. So, your new partner is a bit of a slob. The upside is that you don't spend all weekend spring-cleaning. So, they're overweight. You get to lie around in bed all Sunday watching black-and-white movies rather than going to the gym. So, they're never back from work till late – at least they will be able to afford a massive Christmas pressie, and it shows they are not lazy.

Chapter Nine

The Flirty 30

more than 29 bits of solid-gold flirting know-how

1. Practise on a Minger

Call us weird, but if you've been out of the flirting game for a while and you need to get your mojo back, then practise. No, not on the mirror – try flirting with someone you're not actually attracted to. Really – the rude bloke behind the counter in the newsagents, the suicidal-looking cashier at your local supermarket. You'll get some much-needed practice in, *plus* you'll seriously make somebody's day.

2. Flirting Has a Bad Rep

It does, though, doesn't it? People tend to associate flirting with couples falling out and getting back at each other; with mind games; or with pissed-up fumblings at the office party – red-faced men in polyester suits trying to recover their lost youth. But let's reclaim flirting for what it *really* is – which is fun, an art, a mix of brains, wit and sensuality. How? Well…

3. Four Flirty Moves
(for beginners)

(i) Speaking to the object of your affections, place your hand forwards, palm up. It's a pose that says, 'I'm comfortable with you.'

(ii) During conversation, touch their hand or shoulder when you want to make a point.

(iii) Laugh at their jokes a lot, even if you don't think they're all that funny.

(iv) You're in a noisy place? Then feel free to get up close and personal. The ears are sensitive little organs, so whisper into them.

4. Flirty Facts (one)

The most common mistake people make when flirting is overdoing eye contact (from research conducted by the Social Issues Research Centre). What that means is look, but don't look *too* much – they'll think you're staring at them or that you have boggly eyes.

5. Use Your Voice

Slow it down, take deep breaths.

6. Don't Go Overboard and Scare off Your Prey

Remember that people are much, much more intuitive than we give them credit for. A smile or a tiny brush on the arm is often all it takes for your flirting target to take the bait.

7. Flirty Words (one)

'Why does a man take it for granted that a girl who flirts with him wants him to kiss her when, nine times out of ten, she only wants him to *want* to kiss her?' Helen Rowland

8. Eye Contact

It's easy to go OTT on the old eye contact and end up looking like something in a bad afternoon soap. Get it right, though, and you've mastered the basics of good flirting. First, if you want to establish eye contact with someone it's probably wise to put a bit of space between you – the ancient eyes-across-a-crowded-room cliché is a cliché because, well, it's true. Eye contact up close can be a bit disconcerting and, frankly, creepy. Second, learn to translate that eye language. If you establish eyeball action across the room you're hoping that person will a) blink, then b) drop their eyes before returning the look. If they don't they're either pissed or not interested.

9. Flirty Words (two)

'There are times not to flirt: When you're sick. When you're with children. When you're on the witness stand.' Joyce Jillson

10. Don't Take the Piss Too Much

Flirting usually starts with a bit of light mickey-taking, but remember – it can easily get out of hand if you don't know each other very well. One minute you're chuckling because you've both worn garish clothes, the next you're being restrained by burly men in bomber jackets as you attempt to rip out each other's throats while screaming, '*My* top is loud? At least *I* don't look like a rainbow with a crack habit!'

11. Use Your Instinct

All this stuff is guidelines. There is no substitute for listening to that little voice, so do it.

12. Five Flirty Moves
(intermediate)

(i) While you're chatting, lean in towards them.

(ii) Bite your lip. Very sexy!

(iii) Look for a scar (however small – even a titchy mosquito bite will do) and then show excessive concern while firmly grabbing the area to take a closer look – you have achieved body contact under another guise. Bingo.

(iv) Ask them if it's too hot or cold in the room and put your hands on their cheeks or neck to check.

(v) 'Ruffle' their clothes. This works especially well with a scarf. You grab it and playfully ruffle it under their chin, usually while saying something flirty. Works a treat.

13. Watch the Sexual Innuendo

Everybody has a line. So while you may believe that you're making coy and innocent double entendres, your new friend could think you're a potty-mouthed porno addict. Also, if the innuendo goes too far too soon, well, where do you go from there? Unless you're planning on jumping into bed *that very second*, you may suddenly find yourself in a 'how do you follow that' situation. You've simply run out of things to say to each other.

14. Don't Be a Gossip

A quick and easy way to establish intimacy is to gossip and bitch at other people's expense. Try not to do it, though, however handy a shortcut it seems. What you say can easily be misinterpreted, and it says much more about you than about them anyway. Plus, if you choose your targets incorrectly you could end up slagging off your new friend's mother. And then end up picking broken glass out of your forehead.

15. Keep Your Distance

A bit of leaning and talking into the ear is great, but watch you don't start 'crowding' someone. Not only is it rude but invading someone's personal space is also one sure-fire way to get them desperately seeking the door.

16. Don't Scan the Room

A quick straw poll reveals that the thing people hate most when talking to someone new or indeed old is that person looking around the room. It just appears as though you're searching for someone more interesting to talk to. If you have a good reason to do so – like you really need to spot a pal, or you're checking to see if so-and-so has arrived yet – then just tell the person you're speaking to. Otherwise you'll look like an ignorant git.

17. Get in There

Please don't make the mistake of standing around with a face like a wet Wednesday morning, attempting to look pale and interesting and expecting someone gorgeous to glide up and ask you about Jean-Paul Sartre. Unless you're Audrey Hepburn it isn't going to happen. Enjoy yourself and people will want to enjoy themselves with you.

18. Offer to Get the Drinks

It's always a nice gesture. Ah, but now you're remembering all those times when you went to the bar and returned, only to find the object of your affection deep in conversation with someone else, barely acknowledging you as you handed them a G&T. Well, what better signal do you want? They're just not interested. If, however, you return to find them anxiously awaiting you? Ker-ching!

19. Use Their Name

But don't overuse it, or you'll sound like a salesman.

20. Make Your Compliments Genuine

And you will reap your rewards, dear dater.

21. Be Socially Generous

Should someone else come to join your tête-à-tête, don't freeze them out; include them. Yes, you were really enjoying those special moments before The Gooseberry arrived, but if you make this apparent then you're going to come across as tetchy, paranoid and uptight. Instead, be confident and self-assured; introduce yourself or your new friend. Be welcoming and warm. Chances are The Gooseberry will get the hint and bugger off anyway.

22. Ask Them Their Feelings

No, not deep-down, did-your-parents-show-you-enough-affection feelings. Just get their opinions on stuff: 'What did you think of that?' and 'What do you reckon about this?' Nothing heavy – their expert analysis of the latest episode of *East-Enders* will do – but believe us when we say that people absolutely love being asked their opinions on things. By doing so you will make them feel very, very special indeed.

23. Learn from the Born Flirts

Do you know somebody who is…

a brilliant laugh

always up, bubbly and optimistic

a great listener

at ease with different types of people

great at eye contact

brilliant at making people feel better
about themselves?

In other words, 'a natural' (the utter, utter bastards). Well, these are the people to learn from when it comes to flirting.

24. Smile

Just smile, okay? Nobody ever flirted with a face like a naked gravedigger.

25. Flirty Facts (two)

Women are more likely to attract a man if they send out several flirting signals rather than relying on a single move. (Monica Moore, PhD, psychologist and co-author of the study *Predictive Aspects of Nonverbal Courtship Behavior in Women*.)

26. Six Flirty Moves (expert)

(i) Girls, get the bloke to guard the door to the loo at a party.

(ii) Invent a reason for a big hug.

(iii) If you shake hands then linger over the grip.

(iv) Ladies, pull your hair loose. It's obvious, but he'll love it.

(v) Rub your shoulder like you have a painful neck. Accept any offer of massage.

(vi) Pass by them in a crowded room and touch them as if for support.

27. Flirty Words (three)

'All women are flirts, but some are restrained by shyness, and others by sense.' Samuel Johnson

28. Women are More Intuitive with their Flirting

And miles better at reading it than men. That's a fact.

29. Never Force this Stuff

Just let it flow, okay?

30. Have Fun

Please!

Chapter Ten

Three Days and Counting...

the essential stock-take before your date

Oh bollocks. You've followed all the advice and you've actually *got a date*. That should be a good thing, but it's not, because the last time you went out on a date, George Michael and Elton John were both heterosexual and mobile phones were the size of small houses in Wiltshire. You've lost touch – not just with society, but with yourself too. You're a mess. You've developed a set of personal habits that even disgust yourself and – let's not forget – you haven't got a thing to wear.

What are you going to do?

Calming down would be a good start. And reading on would be a decent next step, because while nobody is suggesting you should turn yourself into the perfect Stepford human being, there are certain, easy steps you can take to – as mother would say – 'make the best of yourself'. Nothing grand; nothing expensive. Let's start with the wardrobe, shall we?

A Question of Clothes
(Ask yourself these and you won't go far wrong – hopefully)

Do You Have a 'Fall-back' Outfit?

Well, you should. This is an outfit that you know looks good, and that is hanging obediently in your wardrobe awaiting you. There will always come a time when you just can't decide what to wear, or you're already late, or you're feeling bloated, or you've just got jam down your other outfit… And that is the time you will do two things. First, you will reach for your fall-back outfit. Second, you will make a mental note to thank us for insisting that you need a fall-back outfit in your wardrobe.

Is Your Outfit Trendy?

If it is, then you need to think very carefully about it. Have you thought? Now think again. Because 99 times out of… well,

99 actually, what is trendy suits nobody – nobody normal anyway. Do you spend your time with people holding your hair back while you vomit a single Ryvita into a basement toilet? Do gay men jab pins into your back while screaming insults at you? Are you conducting an on-off relationship with a pre-pubescent drug addict? If the answers to these questions are 'No', then you're not a model and you're not going to suit what is trendy. Instead, choose clothes that flatter your shape and go with your body type, and always, always go for style over what's 'in'.

Are You Dressing to Suit Your Personality?

Well don't. Your personality should come across in what you say and how you say it. You don't need to semaphore it with your clothes. Only clowns do that.

Are You Dressing Your Age?

Sorry, but if you're in your 40s and you totter up wearing a micro-skirt, then people are going to smirk behind their menus. And here's the real kicker: *they will smirk even if the look really suits you*. Why? Because it's a cruel world, and people – especially women – have to dress their age. Hey, we don't make the rules.

What Are You Saying with Your Outfit?

Yes, so it fits and it looks good on you and people say how great you look in it, but what message is it sending to your date who, remember, doesn't know you at all? The 'sexy' get-up might just look slutty to him. Your best designer clobber may make you look too high-maintenance. These are first impressions we're talking about here. Save the statement gear for one or two dates down the line, when your date is hooked and wriggling...

Do You Dress Appropriately?

For some reason, there's always a girl in the pub dressed like she's going to the gym. Who knows, maybe there are girls in the gym dressed like they're going to the pub. Either way, they've made the mistake of thinking, 'I like these clothes. I like them so much I really don't care where I'm going, I'll wear them anyway.' But then they get sniggered at in books like this, and you don't want that, do you? No. Good. So think about where you're going and match the venue to your outfit.

Do You Go Overboard?

Ladies, there is nothing – *nothing* – men hate more than a woman who is so dolled up she looks like she might break. If you appear too pristine, you might as well wear a sandwich board that says, 'I don't know how to have fun. And I will keep you waiting for two hours while I get ready to go out and not have fun.' If you're the sort of person who flinches slightly when somebody puts their hand too near to your hair, then you're on your way to becoming this woman already.

Do You Dress for Comfort?

No? Well you should, especially if you're a bloke. The most important secret to looking good for a bloke is comfort. If you feel naked without buttons, put on a shirt. If a long-sleeve smart-ish T-shirt and your best jeans make you feel more at home, then wear them. Actually, wash them then wear them. Similarly, fashionable trainers are as good or bad as the shiniest expensive shoes if they make you feel good – as long as they don't smell.

Awkwardness in unnatural threads can heighten any awkwardness felt at an uncomfortable silence during a dinner date. You haven't spent years (or minutes, some of you) building up a wardrobe only to ditch it for the first female to take your fancy in a good while. She will either be smitten with you for who you are, or not at all, and the way you look is part and parcel of that.

Do You Dress Like a Patchwork Quilt?

We've all done it. You have a top that you really, really like. You have a skirt that you really, really like. What do you do? You wear them together. But they don't go together, says a little voice in your head. You ignore that voice because you like these clothes so much they simply must go together. Don't ignore the voice. That's your instinct talking and you must always listen to it.

Are You Over-accessorizing?

It's easy to go bananas on the bits and pieces. Those nice earrings, that great necklace. It's another 'little voice' scenario. Listen to it and don't overdo the accessories. You don't want to look like a pirate, do you?

! **Hot tip:** Trust your instincts and go with them.

Waxing

Ladies, welcome to the waxing dilemma. In other words, the 'when' of waxing. Do it the day of the date and you will be red all over – too long before and you will have five o'clock shadow.

There are bits of both men and women that someone somewhere elected would be better hairless, and now you're being bent into terrible positions and undergoing a considerable amount of agony in an attempt to be more pleasing to the opposite sex. Ultimately it does come down to individual taste, but having a man with a hairless back or a woman with hairless forearms is not essential to a good sex life.

Voice

Obviously, you can't get a voice transplant to get rid of your foghorn/air-raid siren/asphyxiated cat (delete as appropriate), but there are simple things you can do to sound your best. First of all, don't prattle on, even if you think it makes you look cute and kooky and a bit like Julia Roberts in *Pretty Woman*. You're not Julia Roberts (unless you are, in which case, hello there, Julia, hope you're enjoying the book), so just take a deep breath – literal or mental – try and relax and sloooow it down.

Those who have to speak in public say the trick is to slow your voice down so that it sounds unnatural to you. But – crucially – to those listening it will sound measured, deliberate and authoritative. Still paranoid about your dulcet tones? Try these...

- **Try listening to yourself on your voicemail.** How do you sound? As well as keeping your voice slow and measured, think about varying its pitch. There's nothing more boring than a dull monotone.

- **Look at yourself in the mirror as you're talking.** An expressive, open and smiling face is much more attractive than a Botox-fixed mask.

- **Read a book to a mate.** Okay, not the whole book, but a page or so. Get them to give you the lowdown on how you sound. Most people speak either too quietly or too loudly – you want to get it somewhere in between.

- **Still having trouble slowing down?** Take deep breaths. Remember that you're not going to be interrupted or cut off; you won't be competing for airtime with colleagues or a group of mates. This date is strictly one-on-one, so you can afford to take... your... time.

Habits

Sorry, but if you're going to fling yourself back into the dating game, you'll need to do a painful stock-take of the person you've become since you last looked. Whether you've just come out of a long, long relationship, or you've simply been solo for a while, the chances are that you've developed some off-putting, er, 'little habits' during that period. 'Who, me?' Yes, you…

When you're with your pals do you take a call on your mobile without bothering to excuse yourself? What's okay with that rabble won't necessarily be cool with your date.

Perhaps you swear like a squaddie with Tourette's when you're at home. Leave it there, eh? Your vocabulary says a lot about you – how you use it says a lot about your respect for your companion. And that's the fucking truth.

Do you clear your throat too much? Cough a lot? Do you (shudder) clear your nasal passages noisily? You probably don't even know you're doing it, especially if you haven't had a significant other nagging you about it half the time. Ditch it!

Maybe you have words or phrases that you overuse, yeah? Do you know what we mean, right? Get rid…

Let's not labour the point, which is that everybody has habits. Your job is to weed out the bad ones.

Manners

Nobody wants to go out with a pig. You really need to mind your manners, just like your habits, if you're intending to launch yourself on an unsuspecting world. No, we're not suggesting you invest in a copy of Debrett's and a month at a Swiss finishing school; just that you put a bit of thought into… well, into being a bit thoughtful. So…

Try not to get pissed. It's okay if both of you are heading in that direction, but you really don't want to be flying solo, do you?

Gents, fancy 70 trillion Brownie points for doing very little? Then open doors for your date. Men tend to complain that they don't do this because of a 'bad experience' when they were accused of being a sexist pig. Most people (not just women, note) actually like to have a door held open for them. So somebody snapped at you. Once. Five years ago. Get over it.

Make an effort. Sounds obvious, doesn't it? But if you've ever got dressed up for a night out, then turned up to discover that your date hasn't even bothered to brush their hair, then you'll know what we're on about. The not-making-an-effort person was hoping to appear laid-back and cool. But actually they just look like they're smelly, can't be arsed and won't change the toilet roll when it needs doing. It's not a good look.

Again, don't want to hammer the message home here – just think Considerate.

Now, the Body...

Ah well. With three days to go until your date there's not a lot you can do about the extra pounds you've been piling on. But before you reach for the razors, consider this: how much will your potential date care? We can assure you they will not notice or care nearly as much as you will. Absolutely everybody has something about their body they are paranoid about – so remember you are not alone worrying about yours.

The chances are that your date will be no more perfect than you are, so chill out and remember that a bit of confidence makes up for a lot of flabby bits. Put your shoulders back, hold your head up high and tell yourself you are looking hot tonight – it's not a night for body paranoia.

All this really goes back to feeling good about yourself. Just remember: you are not alone in feeling a little imperfect – the right person will find you perfect anyway.

! **Hot tip:** Put your shoulders back – standing up straight makes a huge difference to how your body looks.

Chapter Eleven

Bath or Shower? Condoms or Mace?

all set for your big night out? thought not...

So, it's tonight is it, the big date? Here you are, getting all het up, and the rest of the world is carrying on like it doesn't have a care. How can people carry on oblivious to the fact that tonight you'll undergo an experience like a job interview – only worse? Most job interviews aren't conducted over drinks and dinner, so you don't have the added worry about whether the garlic on the mushrooms will render you unsnoggable. And job interviews don't normally end with one of you wondering whether a kiss is on the cards, and of course if you do, is it time for a bit of tonsil tango or not? Well, not usually anyway…

Yes, a date is much more scary.

So it's time to get a grip, pull yourself together and get ready. Need some help? Happy to be of service…

> ! **Hot tip:** If you're excited about the date, why not use it as a good excuse to spend some money on yourself? A haircut, a new pair of shoes or even a bit of a facial are all good for the soul, if not the pocket, so go ahead and splash out.

The Ultimate First Date Checklist
(Possibly the only date checklist you'll EVER need)

1. Tidy Up

Tidying your flat is a sound plan but try not to look like you were expecting your date to come back. Happening to have a bottle of wine in the fridge and some milk so you can offer them coffee is not a bad move, though. You might want to sober up quickly so make sure there are some carbs in the cupboard – having to run out to the 24-hour garage can ruin the moment somewhat.

2. Sort Your Hair Out

No, not the hair on your head, your – ahem – other hair. Remember the waxing dilemma from the last chapter? Well, if you didn't wax it then you've got to think about it now. As a rule trimming is required, especially if you've got hair sprouting from your ears, nose or elsewhere. Beyond that (i.e. down below) it comes down to a matter of taste. As a general rule the following applies: what most men want in a woman is zero hair on the armpits and legs, and a little topiary around the bikini line. Don't be tempted to whip the lot off just because your last boyfriend liked it – plenty of men are horrified by this.

Typically, what women want in men is less time-consuming and painful. In fact, many women would rather a hirsute man than one looking like a teenager. By the way, don't think we're assuming you're going to end up in the sack here. We're not. Never hurts to be prepared, though, yes?

3. Talk to a Mate

Safety first. Make sure you tell a friend where you're going and with whom (and that you'll call the next day to give them all the juice).

4. Put Your Pants On

Big or small pants? Matching sexy underwear will make you feel much better but will probably encourage you to show it off after a few glasses of wine. Best not to wear your very best undies unless you plan on taking them off.

5. Get Your Look Right

Never wear clothes that are too small – you won't look smaller, just that you can't fit into your clothes. Neither is tonight the night to test out a 'new look' – to really make the most of the date you need to be as relaxed as possible. But, most importantly, you need to be *you*. Keeping up the pretence that you wear six-inch stilettos and a mini-skirt if you are a jeans and boots girl is going to be not only difficult but excruciatingly painful too.

So what *should* you wear? We've conducted painstaking research to come up with a crucial list of image dreams and nightmares. Ignore these at your peril…

Dreams

- **Clean hands, tidy nails** Don't look out the window, gents, we're talking to you. Yes, you whose hands have got phone numbers scrawled in Biro on them, and half a compost heap under your fingernails. Those hands are going nowhere, matey.

- **Fresh, light scent** Men hate overpowering scent on women. And – news just in – women hate overpowering scent on men. Keep it subtle and remember the cardinal rule that just because you can't smell it doesn't mean it's not poisoning the wildlife. That goes for you too, chaps. This may seem obvious but – oh, to hell with it – men, if you could try and be really clean that would be much appreciated. If you wear a cologne then use neutral shower gel or soap. Similarly, there's no point having an expensive eau de toilette if it's fighting a losing battle against Lynx Africa. Choose a deodorant that doesn't leave white marks. Lastly, don't go overboard on the smelly stuff. One squirt will do. Lecture over.

- **Bit of cleavage (not too much)** Do you want to spend the evening talking to the top of his head? Thought not. Oh, and never, ever mix a plunging top with a micro-skirt. Not unless you want to spend the night fending off men in company cars whose wives don't understand them.

- **Closely shaved** Pay attention chaps, this is you again. A note on stubble. If you want to sport designer stubble that's all well and good, but make sure it's proper stubble, please. Don't bother if large patches of your cheeks are smooth as a baby's bum.

- **Clean, white shirt** White-shirt fans are legion, and they're on both sides of the gender divide. Most seem to agree that a bit of a tan works best, though absolutely and categorically not too much *fake* tan. Oh, and be careful if you're planning on having the spaghetti. Actually...

  > **! Hot tip:** What are we thinking? Never have spaghetti on a date, whether you're wearing a white shirt or not.

- **Clean hair** Dirty, straggly hair might look okay if you're a rock star junkie, but you're not one of those, are you? No, you're you, and we promise that you look so much better with nice, clean hair.

- **Clean teeth** Yucky teeth are something not even rock star junkies can pull off with any style. If they are stained brown with nicotine, go to the dentist right now for all our sakes. Check, check then check again that you don't have today's lunch still hanging around in your gnashers. If your date is after work then our advice is take your toothbrush to the office. On that note, here's another tip...

  > **! Hot tip:** Lay off the peanuts. They leave all kinds of debris in your mouth and get between your teeth.

- **Good shoes** Some people have a 'thing' about shoes, so bear in mind you may well be judged on them. As a rule, keep them clean, simple, stylish and well made.

- **Cool and unruffled** You've walked into a hot restaurant from a cold night outside. You're nervous and anxious about the evening ahead. Yes, the chances are you may perspire (or 'glow' if you went to finishing school). The answer to this age-old problem is to layer. In other words, make sure you can take enough clothes off so as not to get hot under the collar.

- **Good posture** Sit or stand up straight. It not only shows confidence but you'll also thank us in old age when you don't have to pay for a chiropractor. Good posture also happens to make absolutely anyone look more attractive.

Nightmares

- **Lots of jewellery** Is it just us or has society gone jewellery mad? The whole world looks like it's sponsored by Ratners. Sigh. Just go easy on the baubles – please. And that goes double for chaps. Take sovereign rings, for example... and put them in the bin.

- **Too much fake tan** See above. For some reason it's become socially acceptable (nay *preferable*) to walk around looking as though you've just had a fresh coat of varnish. Sure, a light spray gives you a confidence boost, but go easy on it...

- **Overdone nails** Yes, we're talking to you with the American flag painted on your nails. You know that's an hour of your life you'll never get back, don't you?

- **Hair gelled like plastic lego trees** Sorry to shatter the illusion, but Barbie's Ken never actually got any – neither are you likely to with half a tub of gel on your head. And woe betide you if it rains...

- **Anoraks and cycling shorts** Here's a crazy plan, and it might just work. Instead of walking into the date and stripping off your retina-hurting fluorescent gear while simultaneously wiping sweaty hair away from your forehead and complaining about the traffic, why not try changing before the date? Because yes, yes, we're all very impressed that you've 'gone green' and now cycle everywhere, but the fact is, it ain't pretty.

- **Badges** A wristband from a festival you went to three weeks ago. A stamp on your hand from last night's 'really cool' indie event. That's just showing off about a club that your date doesn't belong to.

- **Designer logos** Any item of clothing where a designer logo is a 'feature' just has try-hard written all over it. And that goes double for clothes branded with the logos of famous sports cars.

- **Frozen turkey flesh showing** You know, when it's gone all blue and white. Put some more clothes on or you'll catch your death.

- **Football tops** Yes, men, we're talking to you. They look awful and what's more, if you wear a football shirt to *a date*, then God only knows what you wear round the house.

> **! Hot tip:** Get a sartorial second opinion. Preferably from the opposite sex if that is who you are trying to appeal to (and siblings/parents/exes don't count). A friend can be a great ally in these situations, so heed their advice, but don't follow it blindly as you might be in danger of becoming their latest action figure. Where they can be of great help is with the final touches, the attention to detail.

6. Pack Some Mints

Always take a packet of mints on a date as a quick breath-freshener. Not chewing gum, as you'll need to find somewhere to put it, plus there is something about people endlessly masticating that sends out the wrong impression, like you might as well shave half off your IQ. Mints it is.

7. Wear Comfy Shoes

Yes, we sound like someone's mum, but it would be a shame to cut short a romantic small-hours walk because of oozing blisters.

8. Take Some Cash

Even if you normally wave your card around, it's worth having some cash on you – just in case. This is one night you don't want to be standing in a cash machine queue while the person in front of you checks their balance, then orders a statement, then tries another card, checks their balance again, orders a statement and then requests a receipt but leaves without taking it. Look, if you're going to request a receipt, at least have the good grace to take the bloody thing.

9. Don't Go Out Boozing the Night Before

However hardcore you might be, your face will still be puffy and you will smell like a tramp for 24 hours after your bender.

10. Plan Your Journey to and from the Date

It's always worth it – just to avoid last-minute disasters and safety issues.

11. Charge Your Mobile Phone

And check you've got plenty of credit, too. Sod's law you'll need to use it if you don't.

12. Condoms

Take them whether you have something to put them on or not. We won't bother listing the reasons why – we all know them.

! **Hot tip:** The most important thing for body and mind is to get a good night's sleep beforehand. Your skin looks its best, your mind works its best and you will be better company.

Okay, are we ready? Good. Then let's go...

Chapter Twelve

Bowling, Cinema, Shark-fishing?

you've got a date – where are you going to go?

Now it gets really interesting – and fun. You've got a date, so you're about to meet someone totally new. On the one hand you might dislike each other intensely, but on the other... wow. Wherever you go on this date, better make it somewhere good...

Restaurant

✓ **Yay!** You get to eat, and everybody loves eating.

✓ **Yay!** There is rarely any shortage of conversation at a restaurant. Note the use of the word 'rarely'. That's us covering our asses for when you find yourself sitting opposite Mr or Ms monosyllabic.

✗ **Nay!** Things can go wrong at restaurants. You can think you're ordering tiramisu and end up with taramasalata. You can get the aforementioned taramasalata down your top. You can burst out laughing and accidentally spray your date with taramasalata, while simultaneously getting taramasalata up your nose. Unable to breathe, you can be in need of the kiss of life, but the only person qualified to administer it is allergic to taramasalata. You can be the first person ever to drown in taramasalata.

✗ **Nay!** There's always the potential problem of whether the man pays or you go Dutch. It's a worldwide problem – even in Holland they worry about going Dutch. But don't worry, we'll come to that...

Your Place

✓ **Yay!** Your gaff, your rules. But NOT EVER on the first few dates. You don't know if they are a nutter yet. Don't even start the date at your place. Neutral ground is best, both for the first meeting and the first date.

✓ **Yay!** Assuming you're cooking, you get to eat *exactly* what you want, when you want it, on plates you've chipped with your own fair hands. Your date gets to see the real you.

✗ **Nay!** You have to go tonto on the tidying-up, because they *will* notice that fluff-coated sock beneath the television. They *will* sit down, say, 'Oops,' reach behind them and pull something unpleasant from beneath your sofa cushions.

The Pub

✓ **Yay!** It's casual, it's relaxed, and unless you're meeting in a deserted hamlet somewhere in Somerset, there will be plenty of activity. If needs be, you can organize some friends to 'coincidentally' be in the pub at the same time.

✓ **Yay!** There's booze at pubs. News just in: booze is a great social lubricant, and before long you'll both be getting on like the proverbial property inferno.

✗ **Nay!** Late-breaking news: booze helps us get rid of our inhibitions, along with our clothes, our money, our sense of shame…

✗ **Nay!** Come on, this is a first date. Can't we think of somewhere a little more imaginative than the boozer?

The Cinema

✓ **Yay!** You get to see a film, which is nice.

✓ **Yay!** Er… You get to eat popcorn?

✗ **Nay!** It's dark, so you won't see your date and your date won't see you, which means Chapter 10 was a waste of your time and ours.

✗ **Nay!** You don't get to talk during a film, do you? You can go for a drink afterwards, of course, and at least you'll have something to talk about…

Bowling/Ice-skating/ Something Else Active

✓ **Yay!** This kind of 'activity date' has an ever-so-slightly *worthy* whiff to it, but in actual fact can be one of the best, simply because you get to do something fun that doesn't involve throwing wine and food down your neck – for once.

✓ **Yay!** If you don't hit it off as lovers, this sort of date is the perfect springboard to make it as friends.

✗ **Nay!** Potential for wrongness on an apocalyptic scale here, especially if you agree to, say, windsurfing when you've never done it before. And you can't swim. You might be a company director with an annual turnover of £3 million, but that won't mean squat when you're being rescued from the middle of a freezing reservoir by a smirking 12-year-old lifeguard.

✗ **Nay!** Again, not much opportunity for social intercourse. Unless you count the three hours spent in A&E.

An Art Gallery

✓ **Yay!** You get to see some good art, plus you will feel incredibly self-righteous as you wander around the gallery, assuming a straight-backed, intellectual air and peering down your nose at the pieces. (Never 'paintings' or 'thingies', note. Stuff in art galleries is always called 'pieces'.)

✓ **Yay!** You can mug up beforehand, wave imperiously at something in the corner and tell your date: 'This piece reminds me of Henry Moore during his bronze period, whereas this piece here has the air of a Picasso, don't you think?'

Meanwhile, if you are deeply puerile you might find a partner in crime to laugh at the rude bits of the statues, but then again we're not sure how many people over the age of 14 are still prepared admit to finding them funny.

✗ **Nay!** If your knowledge of Picasso starts and ends with Paloma's perfumes, or your appreciation of Moore is restricted to Roger's performance in *The Spy who Loved Me*, then you're asking for trouble.

✗ **Nay!** You can't really chat in art galleries. Well, you can, but if you do a phalanx of straight-backed intellectual people will instantly descend upon you and purse their lips, looking as though they're trying to siphon whipped cream through a straw.

A Gig

✓ **Yay!** You get to see a band. You can drink, let your hair down, dance.

✓ **Yay!** You will be pressed up against your date for a good portion of the night. (Needless to say this could so easily be a nay.)

✗ **Nay!** Once again you've got the communication problem. You thought bawling at each other during the warm-up DJ was bad. By the time the support band comes on you're beginning to lose your voice and you've said 'pardon', 'sorry', 'come again' or one of its variants a thousand times. Worse, you've done that thing where the other person has asked you a question, but you didn't hear it so you just nodded and smiled, and now they're looking at you with a blank, enquiring face. It dawns on you that you're going to have to ask them to repeat the question, which makes a complete mockery of your previous nodding and smiling so now you look like a fake and a fraud into the bargain. And then the main act comes on and it gets really bad...

✗ **Nay!** She reckoned on seeing Robbie at Wembley. He thought they might catch Goatwhore at King's Cross Water Rats. You can see where this is going, can't you?

Not a Date

✓ **Yay!** A not-a-date, or an 'undate', is supposed to take the pressure off the date because, uh, it's not a date. The not-date is arranged on a non-dating night like, say, Wednesday and the activity is determinedly un-datey, like shopping, walking the dog or sorting your whites from your darks. The Yay! factor is the lack of the usual datey stress, apparently.

✓ **Yay!** Less will hinge on this kind of date, so if it all goes terribly wrong, nobody loses face, supposedly.

✗ **Nay!** Excuse us, but all that time and effort spent making certain it's not a date – doesn't that kind of make it just as stressy and prepared as an actual date?

✗ **Nay!** Isn't this just a bloody stupid idea?

Last-minute Thoughts

We asked some of our friends for their last-minute date advice. Here's what they came up with...

'Don't be tempted to impress by suggesting somewhere to meet that is "the" place to be. Middle of the road is key – not too expensive, not too scummy. You are meeting a person, not writing a restaurant guide.'

'A simple, quiet bar is a good bet. If you arrange dinner and in the first five minutes you realize you have absolutely nothing in common, you have a fairly painful evening ahead of you.'

'It's a good idea to arrange to meet for just a drink, saying beforehand that you have to be somewhere else at a certain time, which gives you around an hour for the date. And, you can always conveniently 'cancel' your next appointment if you're getting on. If you can't manage to make polite small talk for an hour, even if you never want to see them again, then you are not very nice!'

'Make sure it's not too noisy – you don't want to spend the whole time asking your potential new beau to repeat them-selves, thereby sounding as though you need a hearing aid.'

'Give them a chance – just because as you walk in you don't want to rip their clothes off doesn't mean that you won't have a fun evening. Remember, they might end up your best friend instead of your other half so give it a bit of time.'

'Always offer to buy both of you a drink – to not offer is just tight whether you are a man or a woman, and to buy one just for yourself is unspeakable.'

'Make sure you have plenty of cash – if they don't take cards it doesn't give a good impression not to be able to pay for a couple of beers.'

'Have a plan as to how to get out of there if you do happen to get on well.'

'If you are a man, remember that good old-fashioned chivalry is NOT dead. You have to pay – that's just bad luck. We have to give birth – that's also just bad luck. Don't expect a second date if you haven't paid for the first one. Going Dutch is acceptable if you have no intention of this ever being a romance.'

'If you just had a salad for lunch then eat something before meeting and pouring an oversized glass of vino down your throat – you need to be armed with your brain on a first date. This also has the advantage of enabling you to order light if you go on to dinner, rather than looking like you're a food Hoover.'

'If you're online dating, set up a "non-date" first, like coffee. If it goes well, then set up the actual date.'

'If you're dating someone you kind of know then go for dinner – but meet somewhere first to get rid of your nerves.'

Now go!

Chapter Thirteen

G Is for Gulp...

the a to z of essential first-date ammo

A Is for Alcohol

Don't go overboard on the booze, obviously. This is a lot more difficult than it sounds; you're going to be nervous so the natural tendency is to start throwing back the wine. But if you do, and even if it's the only time you've been drunk in the past two years, your date will still go away thinking you're a high-maintenance lush at best – you don't know this person, remember. The aim is not to be on your 'best' behaviour – that's just dull – but imagine how you'd feel if the shoe were on the other foot and before you knew it your date was streaking down the high street and trying to snog a police horse.

... and for Age

Chances are you already know the age of your date – or at least have a good idea. If not, please be subtle about finding out. There's something intimidating about a stranger who demands to know how old you are. Men, with their tendency towards a love of statistics, are particularly bad at doing this. And women, with their tendency towards hating it when people ask their age, *hate it*.

So, ask them their favourite pop song. Is it 'Take My Breath Away' or 'I Predict a Riot'? Were they wearing granddad shirts and paisley waistcoats when they were young, or hoodies? What were they drinking the first time they ever got drunk: Watney's Red Barrel or an alcopop? You get the picture.

B Is for Be Prepared

Providing you've had at least a cursory scan of the preceding chapters, you should already be prepared for your big night. If not? Oops.

... and for Bless You

When you sneeze, does your date say 'bless you'? If the answer is yes, that's a very good sign. It means they're caring, considerate and thoughtful. Either that or they've read this book, too.

C Is for the Chase

There is a lot to be said for 'the chase'. Remember the old Groucho Marx quote: 'I'd never want to join any club that would have me as a member.' Relationships work along similar lines (up to a point, obviously), and people will instinctively shy away if they think it's all too easy. Give your date something to aspire to – you, in other words. It's not a case of playing hard to get, but neither do you want to lay it on a plate for them...

... and for Critics

Whatever you do, don't criticize, analyse or second-guess. Again, men are the culprits here, and they're especially guilty when it comes to ordering food. Here's a hint, chaps: if a woman wants your advice on what to order, *she will ask for it*. If she doesn't understand the menu, you may think it's harmless teasing to point it out – she won't. Equally, if you're on the receiving end of criticism from someone you've only just met then take note. If they're criticizing you now – with the relationship only hours old – imagine what they'll be like in six months' time. Shudder.

... and for Cutting Your Losses and Leaving

Sally's story: 'I'd like to take you out for dinner,' said Dave, my exciting new mysinglefriend.com boy. 'Somewhere nice in Notting Hill?' he suggested. Sounds promising, I thought – I'd been chatting with Dave for quite a while and we seemed to have a really good rapport going. Cheeky banter, lots of flirting, and from the photo he looked gorgeous.

Yes, I was late, but no amount of apologizing seemed to suffice. On being asked if I was hungry (which I was – very) he told me that he'd had a big lunch so didn't feel like eating, and anyway the restaurant was far too expensive and he didn't want to spend that much money. Hmm…

After a few paltry attempts at small talk he began a mini onslaught of insults – ranging from quite a few references to the fact I was three years older than him (this apparently made me a 'very old bird') to the spectacular, 'You'd look better in the dark than in the light; Top Shop changing room for instance.'

At this, I admitted defeat and left, slightly traumatized.

D Is for... Doubling Up with Laughter

Okay, not doubling up exactly, but laughing, chuckling, giggling, smiling. The aim of the game here is to have a good time, plus – and this is the nice bit – you will be about a thousand times more attractive if you're enjoying yourself.

E Is for Exuding Confidence

Confident is sexy. Be at ease with yourself, relax and have a good time. Note of caution, though: don't substitute confidence for arrogance.

... and for Eye Contact

Now's the time to put some of that body-language bollocks into practice. Good luck...

F Is for Friends

Ask about your date's mates. You can tell a lot about a person from their friends. Do they have mates they made at school? Do they have any exes hanging around? Do they have plenty of friends of the opposite sex? This kind of information will reveal far more about the person than they ever would.

... and for Fibbing

Phil's story: 'I had been email-chatting to a lovely-looking girl named Cathi for some time. From her picture and her emails she seemed to be the kind of girl I was looking for, a bit of a catch: slim, very attractive and a lovely smile. We decided to go on a date and I arranged to pick her up one Friday night.

As it was summer and scorching hot, the front door to Cathi's maisonette was open. I knocked and a voice from upstairs shouted for me to go up.

I peered up the stairs and the first thing I saw was a skirt. A big skirt. In fact it was a huge skirt! Cathi had piled on the pounds, so much so that I think she had been prescribed cakes as a cure for it. The skirt didn't so much have a size as its own postcode.

Now let me get this straight – I am not perfect. I know I have my faults. But Cathi was so different from her picture that if I'd sold her I'd have been prosecuted under trade descriptions. The moral of the story? Recent pictures, please!

... and also for 'Fluffy' People

You know the old saying: 'You're not fat, you're just fluffy'? It means that 'fat' – as in the insulting, pejorative term that gives supermodels sleepless nights – is all in the eye of the beholder. If you're a rounder, fluffier person, then despite what the weekly magazines would have you believe, you're still a gorgeous sex machine. Sure, when you're playing the dating game you might want to steer clear of body-fascist body-builders who spend their lives in the gym smearing baby oil on themselves; but then everybody else wants to steer clear of those people, too. Why? Because they only love themselves...

G Is for Goodbyes

The farewell. Do you kiss or not? And what on earth do you say? Well, if you had a really good night then our advice is not to mess around: tell them you did. Chances are they had a good time, too, and were wondering who was going to be the first to say so. Then leave, and don't set up the next date on the spot. Why? Well, you've had a couple of glasses of wine, haven't you? Your judgment's a wee bit impaired. Why not sleep on it and see how you feel in the morning?

That's if it goes well. Ah, but what if you'd rather scoff the contents of an ashtray than spend another second in the company of this person – this human incarnation of the colour beige? Then it gets a tad more tricky. It's time to put on your best businesslike face, extend your arm for a formal handshake and say, 'It was very nice to meet you. Thank you for the evening.' On no account kiss them, not even a mwah-mwah air-kiss. They should get the message.

H Is for Having a Bloody Good Time

If you leave this book with one message it should be that dating is fabulous and fun. It's not punishment. It's not homework. It's not a necessary evil to get down the aisle. When you're single, you have no idea how much old-time couples secretly envy your lifestyle. Why? Because you're going on dates and *having a good time*. And if you're not, why not?

I Is for Interrupting

Your date speaks… really… really… slowly. Or, they have this habit of making a point then making it again, except using different language. In other words, they say something and then just repeat themselves. They've made their point twice but then they make it a third time. It's annoying, isn't it? And there's you desperate to jump right in and move the conversation forwards to a point where you're not stuck in what feels like Groundhog Date...

But you don't. Because butting-in is perhaps the most common mistake people make when meeting each other for the first time. And boys, you're especially guilty of this. You may be desperate to make your point; you may be frustrated at the lack of conversational progress, but interrupting is impolite and women loathe it.

... and for Insulting Your Date

Tonia's story: I went on a date with a guy after a hard day at work. Because I was tired I seemed to develop verbal diarrhoea, to the point where he actually said, 'Can I just finish my story?'

I could feel myself talking over him but couldn't stop. And at one point I remember saying, 'Can you handle yourself in a fight?' I don't know what came over me.

J Is for Judgment

On a first date, do your best to disengage the bit of your brain that makes snap judgments about the people you meet. It's difficult – almost impossible, in fact – but human nature dictates that we 'decide' about people pretty sharpish, and you could end up writing off your date before it's even begun. So, give them a chance. That said, there are times when you should make a snap judgment and get out of there, quick. These include...

When he turns up wearing a T-shirt with the slogan, 'It ain't gonna suck itself'.

When she rolls up her sleeve to show you her track marks and says, 'All I need is two grand for the rehab...'

When they are sick into their napkin and reassure you 'It's nothing serious, just a slight bile problem...'

K Is for Kissing

Don't mercy-kiss is all we ask. Otherwise, go with the flow.

L Is for Your Life Story

Don't tell it. Not unless you're keen to be shortlisted for the International Masterbore Competition. It's not that your life story is dull – it isn't. It's just that life stories take a long time to tell, and too often the teller can get carried away. Other time-sucking dull-a-thons to avoid include relating the plot of a film you've recently seen or – worse – describing a dream you had once. Nightmare, more like.

... and for Listening

Hopefully you were listening when we told you about the importance of being a good listener. Now's your chance to prove it. Being listened to is not only very flattering and really quite sexy, so your date will feel great, but if you're listening properly you should also be learning lots about them.

M Is for Mobile

Turn it off, or set it to vibrate if you must have it on. It's basic manners, this, and if your date hasn't done the same thing, then take a long, hard look at this person. One minute you're forgiving them for taking a call at the table; the next they're breaking wind in your face and flicking bogies into your muesli. Too late comes the realization, 'I'm going out with an utter pig.'

N Is for Name

Their name – it's worth saying. People like to hear their own name. Oh, and please, please remember your date's name.

It is crap to the power of a trillion to forget it. It's even worse to forget your date's name and then excuse yourself by saying you're terrible with names.

O Is for Ogling

If we said don't ogle other people when you're on your date you'd laugh and tell us not to be so condescending – of course you wouldn't ogle other people on your date. But people do it. And weirdly enough, they do it not because they actually fancy the person they're ogling, but to signal to their date what a sexual animal they are. 'Check me out. I'm caged, ready to go. Rarrgh!' Or they do it because they want their date to feel a teensy bit jealous. Well, both are rubbish reasons. Don't ogle. Instead, concentrate on your date.

P Is for Paying Compliments

Only if you really mean them, mind. And if you don't – do make it sound, ahem, heartfelt.

... and for Paying the Bill

Men – unless she absolutely insists and it looks like things are about to get awkward – it is your job to pay the bill. That's just the way it is.

... and for Pet Names when We've Only Just Met

Babe. Mate. Pal. Buddy. Darling. Love. Bugger. Off.

Q Is for Questions

Ask them. And try to make sure you're asking 'open' questions, which means your date can't answer just 'yes' or 'no', and it may sound obvious but *listen* to the answer.

> **Closed question:** 'It's been really hot today, hasn't it?'
> **Open question:** 'How do you cope in this kind of weather?'

R Is for Realistic

Many people have idealized notions when it comes to looks, relationships and the type of person they want to meet. But the reality is that nobody's perfect – not you nor anybody you will meet. Don't chase an ideal.

S Is for Standards

You could be married tomorrow if you lowered your standards enough. So don't.

... and for Shopping-list Dates

Fi's story: My date and I meet for coffee and the conversation seems to go reasonably well until he slips in what I call his 'shopping list'.

'So, Fi, are you tactile?'

'Sometimes.'

'I mean, if I were washing up, would you walk past and squeeze my bottom?'

'I might do. It depends.'

'Do you throw things? I mean, if you got angry would you throw something at me?'

'Erm... well, if you really were bang out of order, then perhaps.'

'I always do the *Sunday Telegraph* crossword and my girlfriend has to be okay with this because when I've finished I like to have sex.'

Ding dong. This is where I decide it's time I headed off, so I make some excuse about things to do at home and we leave.

'So,' he says, 'I can't really tell if you like me or not. I really fancy you. Perhaps you can let me know tomorrow by 11am if you're interested or not?'

'OK,' I say.

Just as we reach the corner of my road, he looks me up and down and says, 'Yep, you look a good height. Yes, I like your height. That's fine.'

T Is for Timekeeping

Better late than never? No. Better have a bloody good excuse if you're ever late. There are people who claim they can never get anywhere on time, as though it's some kind of affliction for which they should be pitied. Mysteriously, these people are never late for job interviews or football matches or the beginning of *EastEnders*. Once again, it's a manners issue. Remember the mobile, the farting, the bogies in your muesli...?

U Is for Unreasonable Imperfections

Don't be too picky, in other words. We've heard of people dumping otherwise perfect dates for crimes such as...

- having toes a bit like fingers
- eating slightly too loudly
- breathing in a funny way
- coughing weirdly
- some snot poking out of their nose when they laughed – once

More often than not, picky deal-breakers like these say more about the hang-ups of the person doing the dumping than the poor girl or guy with toes like fingers.

V Is for Valid Topics of Conversation

Anything goes, of course. Who are we to tell you what you can and can't talk about on a first date? Here's a short selection of first-date topics we respectfully suggest you avoid, though...

Your ex.

Stuff you like doing in bed.

Stuff you used to like doing in bed with your ex.

Your last doctor's appointment.

Money.

The details of your last break-up.

The lingering feeling you have that you were not shown enough affection as a child and how you think this may explain some of the emotional problems you have now.

The suspicion that you're being followed.

Moans and grumbles (especially about the waiting staff if you're at a restaurant).

Other dates you've been on recently.

Any 'commitment issues' you have.

Babies. And that would include nieces and nephews you adore.

Still, remember to give a little of yourself – it's always a good idea to open up a bit if you want someone else to do the same.

... and also for Very Strange Things to Say on a First Date

Glen's tale: I took this girl out for a date in Bedford-shire, and it was going okay. The conversation was good, and then she asked what I did for a living.

'I am a Sales Manager for a company that sells corporate uniforms,' I replied.

'Oh,' she said, 'I love uniforms. I have two: Miss Air Hostess and Miss Whiplash but they're only for use in the bedroom.'

Maybe a little too much information for the first date?

W Is for What You Want

Dates are often compared to job interviews; they're both situations where you're trying to give a good account of yourself. But remember, it's not just you 'on show' like some kind of competition pony – you also need to make sure that your date is the person you want to be with. If they are – go for it!

... and also for the Weird People to Watch Out for

Claire's story: After years on the 'single mum' shelf and with two glasses of red on board, I followed my pal's recommendation and went online.

Hesitantly I created my profile. After hours of debating whether 'attractive-ish' made me seem arrogant, I declined the image-loading section. The next day the worldwide web replied. It had scanned the *whole* cyber-universe and returned mail from interested parties. Among them was an ex from my school days some 20 years ago; a man who wanted to meet me in a lay-by to watch me pee; and a man with a glass dining table that apparently needed decorating with my faeces!

I've since found mysinglefriend.com

X Is for Exes

Even if you employed a hit man to deal with your ex and have been supplied with video evidence of the execution, guess what? Your ex still isn't out of your life for good. One way or another, they are the reason you're on this first date and, like it or not, their spirit lingers on. So here's the thing. First, don't talk about your ex, and certainly not unless you're specifically asked. If you are, try not to get too detailed about the relationship or the reasons for the break-up. But – and here's the sneaky thing – do as much digging as you can about your date's last break-up. Hopefully they'll be less circumspect than you and will give you the juice on their last relationship. What they say will be very enlightening as to what they're expecting – or hoping for – from their next relationship, plus it will give you clues about their personality.

'We wanted different things,' for example, shows that your date is no walkover, while 'It was moving too fast,' suggests your date doesn't like jet-propelled relationships so you should take it easy with them.

One more thing on exes: try not to compare your date with your ex. If you do, maybe you haven't moved on. And perhaps you should.

Y Is for Yourself
(as in, be yourself)

Well, sort of. Nobody is suggesting you tell your date that traumatic tale about your childhood teddy – the one that always leaves you in tears. What you need to be is a version of yourself that you really, really like: the Hollywood movie version; the cool version; the friendly and entertaining bit of you that comes out to play every now and then. Hand in hand with this goes not pretending to be something you're not. As in, don't tell porky pies about yourself in order to impress your date – even little things like whether you like football or not. This is for two reasons: 1) the porkies will come back to bite you at some point in the future, and 2) you're not being yourself if you're fibbing, are you?

Z Is for Zzz

And all the sleep you're going to have to catch up on if the date goes really well. Ahem.

Chapter Fourteen

'I Think I Hate You'

the shit sandwich and other date-exit strategies

Okay, you're on your date in the pub or restaurant (or ice-skating rink or... just go to Chapter 12, okay?) and things are going pear-shaped, to say the least. For a start you walked in, clapped eyes on your date and they looked nothing like your friend said they would, their photo suggested or you imagined from their emails. Or if you've met them before then they've changed somehow – maybe you were wearing the old 'beer goggles' last time round? Either way, looks-wise they're not up to scratch. Worse, they've turned out to have the conversational skills of a sloth on Prozac. And as for chemistry, there is none, which means there will be no biology either.

You are in dating hell.

Or maybe not *hell* as such. Perhaps all their bits and pieces are in the right place and they can hold a conversation but... it's just that this person is not for you.

That being the case, it's no biggie: it's just life's love lottery giving you the wrong numbers again, not even a bonus ball. But if they seem interested and you're not, they're going to need handling just as carefully as the pests and social throwbacks. In this world there are goodies and baddies – you don't want to be unkind to one of the goodies, do you?

The Flattery Battery

An ancient technique used by dating ninja is to literally praise your date out of your life. It's called the flattery battery and the idea is that your date floats away on a cloud of such fulsome eulogy they hardly even notice they've been given the old heave-ho. So, tell them they are...

Sweet If you're a girl, that is. Blokes will say they hate being called sweet, but secretly they love it.

Funny Everybody wants to be funny. If you've been doing your job properly you will have been laughing like a drain at their every utterance. 'Oh, stop it,' you can gush, 'you're *killing* me.'

Clever Wow. You can do *that?* Crikey, don't you know a lot about *that*.

Stylish Tell them they look great, even if they're dressed like something out of mum's Grattans catalogue circa 1982.

Cool Being cool is the unarticulated desire of every single person under 60 in the Western world.

And then say… 'But I can't see us going out really.' Because you're complimenting your date while also letting them down gently, they leave with their self-esteem still firmly in place.

From the even higher order of the dating ninja comes this extra bit of letting-down-gently advice…

The Shit Sandwich

The idea of the shit sandwich is that you put your marching orders between two bits of such shiny praise that they will love you forever and completely forget that in fact they're as obsolete as Betamax videos. So, you start with the flattery battery, deliver your no-future blow and then follow it up with another head-swelling line, preferably something like, 'Can I give your number to a friend of mine? You two would be perfect together,' or something similar.

They're Not Taking No for an Answer Here...

Your subtle hints, flattery batteries and shit sandwiches just aren't finding their target. Why? Because this person has an ego the size of the Heathrow extension. People with big egos are famously poor at picking up hints. They will refuse to believe that anybody could possibly be immune to their tales of 'pulling down three mil' or ascending Everest for Rupert's stag night, wearing only their Y-fronts. Their idea of heaven is a BMW with a big mirror in it. They just don't do rejection.

Two options for this person, then. Either be so firm that they can't fail to get the message, in which case they will think you're weird, highly strung or definitely 'batting for the other team', or you can play to the stands. In other words, feed their ego by telling them they're simply too much for you – they're the bomb and you're just not ready for that much bombness in your life. Whatever you choose to do, don't make it subtle.

Lastly, of course, you could go down the old 'I want to get married and have lots of babies right now' route. Big-ego types are never ready to settle down. Not when there are more 'mils' to be pulled down, more stag nights to go on and even bigger Beamers to buy.

And Now They're Really Getting on Your Nerves...

Do you walk? Do you grab your stuff, make like a tree and leave? Or do you stick it out till the bitter end, at which point you're *still* going to need an exit strategy of one kind or another? Well, there's a line, and only you will really know whether or not your date has crossed it. In our experience, though, walking out is pretty much a last resort. When should you? Examples please...

Walkies? Your date takes a photograph of your food.

Stay? It's weird, it's odd but it could be quirky, endearing and eccentric. And perhaps your date is an obsessive compulsive, or has other psychiatric issues that you might exacerbate by walking out on them. Give them a break.

Walkies? Your date asks you if you've considered becoming a drug mule, and do you have a passport?

Stay? Woah, they may be kidding, and you're going to feel pretty dumb if they burst out laughing just as you're lunging for your jacket. Also, they could be winding you up so you're anecdote

ammo for when they next see their
mates. Don't give them a good ending.

Walkies? Your date says they
thought you would be thinner and taller,
and is that your own hair? And have
you ever considered augmentation?

Stay? Now we're moving into abuse
and harassment country and you don't
stand for that. Or to put it another way –
you do stand for it. You stand and walk
out. But try not to storm out, much as
you'd like to. If your date's picking on you
like this, it's because they're a shitbag
and they want to provoke a reaction
from you. So no chucking wine over
them, no shouting or sudden movement –
in fact, nothing that will make the pair of
you the centre of attention. That's what
they want. Calmly collect your stuff,
thank them for the drink and leave, head
held high. Ignore the inevitable, 'What?
What did I say?' as you leave. It's just
another attempt to get a rise out of you.
They're not worth it, and with any luck
they have a future of drowning slowly in
sewage ahead of them.

Walkies? There is an incident
involving some of the more unpleasant
bodily fluids.

Stay? Get out of there.

If things have really gone so badly you want out of there then the best thing to do is have a strategy (or lie, as it's sometimes called). Excuse yourself to take a phone call then come back saying you're sorry, but you've been called away on a work or family matter. Don't go into why. Unless your date plays thicko for England they're going to suss you haven't *really* been called away, and either they'll be secretly relieved that the suffocating deadlock of this Chinese water-torture date has finally been broken, or they'll sit and silently seethe. You don't care one way or another. You're out of there.

You've Invited Them Home

- **You did what?** Later, you will mentally beat yourself up for making a date-mistake that's such a schoolboy error it should have muddy knees and a satchel. It was dumb, you won't do it again in a hurry, but now you *have* done it, what the heck are you going to do? Any vibes that the night was a total disaster have been completely lost on this schmuck. They're sitting on your sofa; they're looking smug; they're already thinking about contraception and whether they can get a late bus, or stay the night and go straight to work.

- **You need to get rid of them** Assuming they've come back for coffee, get that cup out of their hands quick. Yawn, glance at your watch, tell them what a busy day you have tomorrow. Start fluffing sofa cushions and tidying up, do the dishes – anything to convince them that you are winding down and you're doing it alone.

  If that doesn't work, invent a sibling – or better still, a parent – whom you're expecting any minute. Er, they were getting a late train and should be in a cab about now. They've only just been released – something like that.

  And when, at last, they get the message and leave, tell yourself you will never, ever invite a failed date back to yours again. It's always better to risk being a bit of a swine and be firm with them than to place yourself in a situation where you have an unwanted stranger in your home.

The Kiss

The biggie. Do you or don't you? Well, this date hasn't gone well, has it? You'd sooner undergo experimental rectal surgery than see this person again, so it's a no-brainer – of course you don't kiss this person. Ideally, as we've said before, the way to end the date from south of hell is to shake their hand – as formally as you can – thank them and skedaddle.

Trouble is, they really want to kiss you. Either because they do actually want to kiss you, or because they've somehow got hold of the idea that a kiss is how dates should end, and not to kiss would be wrong, a crime against nature and all that makes us civilized and separates us from the beasts. Look out for the clues. Is this person...

loitering, with intent to kiss?

gazing into your eyes?

reaching for your hand?

closing their eyes, leaning forwards with their lips puckered, as though about to whistle?

saying, 'Gi's a snog, darling'?

Yes, these are the ever-so subtle and tell-tale signs that your date wants more than a walk home alone. Just shaking their hand isn't going to cut it. Best thing is to give them a quick peck on the cheek. Surprise attack. Get in and out before they've even had a chance to react. That way you've 'done' the kiss, and providing you're lightning-fast they won't have time to try and convert your chaste peck into a lingering drool-a-thon.

Do we need to say that you should never, ever, under any circumstances, up to and including the kidnap of family members, give a bad date a mercy shag? No, we don't.

Chapter Fifteen

'When Should I Call?'

or: how to stop worrying about trivia and go with the bloody flow

So you're going to call your date, which implies your night together wasn't a complete disaster. 'Complete disaster' covers a multitude of sins, obviously, and only you can judge how bad it really was. Are you both alive, for example? Did the evening end with the two of you being pulled apart by riot police? For some people that's a cracking night out. For others, it's a deal-breaker.

Either way, you've decided to see this person again. How badly do you want to see them? Well, that will depend on whether or not you've got Great First Date Syndrome.

What's that? Step behind this screen and we'll show you the symptoms…

Great First-date Syndrome

'Ex? What Ex?'

Whether you were the dumper or the dumpee, chances are you were still wandering around thinking about your ex the whole time. Were you right to dump them? Is there any chance of you getting back together? Will they call? Should you call them? Will you be friends?

You know the kind of thing we mean.

A great date is one that takes a big broom to the inside of your head and sweeps all of that stuff aside. Suddenly, you don't want to get back with your ex because there's this bright and shiny new thing on the horizon and you've just had the most brilliant date.

You Can't Stop Thinking about the Date

There was the bit where the waiter nearly slipped over and a bit of calamari landed on the tablecloth. How you both laughed. Or, what about when you were walking home and you almost fell on your heels and he reached out an arm to steady you?

A good date is one you replay over and over in your head. Not for the bad bits, but for those moments when you both burst out laughing at the same thing, or suddenly discovered you had the same person in common, or realized you'd been at the same gig at exactly the same time and could well have been standing next to each other, or... You get the picture. And not only are you thinking about the evening, but...

You Can't Get Them Out of Your Head

Since the date you've thought about little else but your new friend. Their smile. Their laugh. The way they held their wine glass. The way they walked across the pub. You've found yourself talking about them to work colleagues, even when the conversation doesn't warrant it, like when someone asks you, 'Do you want some more Post-It notes from the stationery cupboard, Jane?' And you reply, 'Great, thanks. I could do with one to write down John's number in case my mobile accidentally drops out of my jeans pocket and falls down the loo, which is what happened to John's sister when she was in France last year. He told me about it in Ricardo's over calamari, and did I tell you what happened when the waiter almost tripped over? A bit of calamari landed on the tablecloth and God, it was so funny...'

'Yes. Yes, Jane, you did. I'm off to the stationery cupboard now. I might be a while. A couple of days, maybe...'

Which, incidentally, is another sure sign you had a brilliant date. Your friends, family and work colleagues have started rolling their eyes when you talk about it. It's called Mate's Great Date Fatigue, and untreated it can lead to Brilliant Relationship Tedium, Marriage Preparation Weariness and then, alas, to New Baby Boredom. But hey, they're just jealous because, unlike you, they haven't just had a great date.

Stuff You Normally Find Annoying Was Cute in This Person

Usually, it drives you up the wall when somebody has that high-pitched, braying laugh that sends dogs running from the room and sets off car alarms. Normally, the one thing you absolutely cannot *stand* is when a person says, 'Do you know what I mean?' every 20 seconds.

But it was different with this person, it really was. Yes, they did have *that* laugh but somehow it seemed to tinkle, charmingly; more importantly they were laughing at the things you said, which made you feel good about yourself. And anyway, only a couple of car alarms went off.

Equally, they did say, 'Do you know what I mean?' at least three times a minute but you know what? They just wanted to make sure that in their enthusiasm to tell you a story they hadn't missed out any important details. It wasn't an annoying habit; they were just being considerate.

(Incidentally, we're not going to wee on your fireworks by telling you that those habits will eventually revert from Cute to Annoying, because you're still basking in the glow of a great first date and we don't want to spoil it for you.)

There Was Definite Chemistry There

During the date you seemed to be on the same wavelength, you laughed at the same things, had the same opinions – all of which are good signs that the pair of you are going to be seeing each other again. But was there something else? Dare we say it, a spark of serious sexual attraction? Something that went a few steps beyond mere eye candy; that had your thoughts hanging around by the bedroom door, looking coy and biting their bottom lip? Grr...

All of a Sudden You've Stopped Looking at Other People

Normally, you're not above checking out members of the opposite sex – of course you're not. The girl who's sometimes at the bus stop, the bloke who works behind the counter at HMV, that woman with the nice smile in the sandwich shop, a guy in the supermarket, a girl you see on the street...

Except, today, the bloke at HMV smiled at you, the girl at the bus stop asked you the time – and you hardly even *noticed them*.

(By the way, the ironic thing is that the HMV bloke and

sandwich shop girl have suddenly started noticing *you*. You've become roughly one thousand per cent more alluring to the opposite sex. Maybe because you look more confident. Or maybe because nature hates us…)

You're Already Looking Forward to Your Next Date

You're itching to see this person again because you want to find out if that mix of chemistry and attraction is going to work a second time around. You want to see them again because you simply can't remember a night when you last laughed so much, or because they expressed an interest in Tom Waits and you've made them a compilation, or because you were arguing about the best-ever episode of *The Simpsons* and you've thought of a few more favourites since then.

Or just because you really, really want to see them again.

A Compromise or Two Suddenly Isn't Such a Big Deal

True, after your last disaster when you spent every Saturday in November and December freezing your tits off in football stadiums, you vowed never, ever to date another football nut. Matter of fact, you even pruned all the football fans from your favourites folder after that. However, somehow one has slipped through and suddenly that vow isn't so important after all. What's a bit of football between friends? Or maybe you have a rule about never dating girls who are taller than you, and it's about to get broken. Perhaps you promised yourself you'd never go out with another solicitor, yet here you are. Finding yourself happy to make a few compromises is a sure sign that this person has you well and truly hooked.

You've Already Started Thinking about Their Christmas Present

Walking past a shop window, something caught your eye that reminded you of a story your date told. Hmm, wonder if they'd like it as a little gift? Or there was that book they mentioned never having read. Perhaps you should buy it for them at lunchtime? See, you're smitten...

They Figure in Your Future Plans

Not big, serious future plans, like marriage or a maternity ward at three in the morning, but the little stuff. There's a party you're going to at the weekend and you're already wondering if they're free. There's Freya's wedding next month and you never know, if things go well you *might* not have to go alone.

Yes, if you've got the symptoms of Great First Date Syndrome it was definitely a good night for you.

Of Course...

You may not have Great First Date Syndrome – like, you still checked out the guy in HMV at lunchtime; you're really, really not sure about that high-pitched laugh – but on the other hand it wasn't a catastrophe: the police weren't called out.

It was just kind of... nice. Okay. Not bad. So-so.

There is potential, in other words, and you're going to have to get in touch to find out whether that potential will be fulfilled.

Getting in Touch...

After deciding you want to see your date again, you then have to think about how and when you intend to contact them.

Many, *many* books have been written advising their readers to wait hours, or days or for a leap year until making their next move. The real answer as to when you should make contact lies in what kind of person you are. Why, for example, should getting in touch quickly put someone off? You could be busy, bored, eager, excited, in a rush, about to travel, needing a date for Friday, or just in demand – all of which are good reasons for not hanging around when it comes to post-date contact. If they like you they'll be delighted you made contact, probably the day after your date. If they don't really think it's going to go anywhere, they can tell you. You can move on.

So what's all the fuss about? To be perfectly honest, we don't know, as it isn't going to make a jot of difference to your relationship (unless it's not going to be a relationship – and making contact too early after your first date isn't going to change that).

Having said that…

Jumping in the second after you've said your farewells and texting, 'When will I see you again?' is not on. It's a doormat question. But you already know that, don't you?

Sending an email or making a phone call while drunk is also a no-no. We've all done it. The night after your great date you're out with a pal and get talking about your new beau. Next thing you know you're texting them with, 'I'm not wearing any underwear,' or ringing them and slurring unintelligible non sequiturs down the phone. Trust us, you will bitterly regret making any conversation that you can't fully recall.

Being ladylike or gentlemanly will always go in your favour.

Girls and boys both feel the same way about 'when to call' and it's a bit foolish if a girl feels she shouldn't make contact – as guys need reassurance too, and the days are gone when the 'chap' did *all* the wooing.

'Help! What Do I Say?'

- **'I had a great time, do you fancy doing that again?'**
  … is an okay line that you may think covers the bases.
  But they could simply reply 'sure' and then not get in
  touch. Now you're lost in the dating wilderness without a
  map. You don't know where you stand, if anywhere. And
  if you slept with them on this first date, they now know
  they can call you for sex. Grrreat. But you wanted a relationship, didn't you?

- **'I had a great time, fancy dinner over the weekend?'**
  … is a far, far better line. The answer, 'I'm busy,' or,
  'I've just got back with my boy/girlfriend,' is an obvious rebuff and you can say you had fun, good luck in
  the future etc., etc… But a reply like, 'Great, what
  about Saturday?' or, 'I'm busy at the weekend, what
  about Tuesday?' leaves you in no doubt. You've set up
  your next date. You now have a few days to feel a bit
  smug.

So what are you waiting for?

Chapter Sixteen

'You Never Blimmin' Did...'

torrid tales from mysinglefriend.com

We asked for your funny, embarrassing or plain weird dating stories, and you did us proud. Space prevents us from printing them all, so here's just a small selection of the ones we received. Some are funny, some are sobering and some just plain bizarre. Have a read, draw your own conclusions and do your best to learn from other people's mistakes!

Sticky Moment

I had been plucking up the courage to ask Liz on a date for ages. She was beautiful, tall and slim with blonde, curly hair and a lovely warm smile. Although she was quiet, I was intrigued by her, and finally after weeks of stuttering and small talk I asked her on a date and she agreed! I was over the moon and remember walking around for the rest of the day like John Travolta in *Saturday Night Fever*. I felt like I was the main man.

So the big day came and I met her at the station so we could catch the train to London. I was nervous as hell and had changed at least twice. Looking at her it was obvious that she was pretty nervous too. Conversation was fairly difficult and uneasy to say the least. Liz, although intriguing and beautiful, was shy so it wasn't long before I ran out of things to ask and finally got down to, 'What bands do you like?'

'No one in particular.'

'Where's your favourite holiday destination?'

'We go camping.'

'Do you have any pets?'

Now this question was the killer to the date and essentially cost me my chances with the lovely Liz.

'Yes, I have a cat.'

'Oh, I love cats,' I replied. It was the truth; we finally had the ice-breaker. Brilliant!

She went on, 'Yes, I love my cat, he always jumps on my bed in the morning and comes all over my face…'

I stopped nodding, the back of my mouth went dry, my face reddened and there I was like a balloon being filled with too much air. I couldn't hold it in anymore and burst out laughing at her obvious poor choice of words.

She looked at me. 'What's funny? Why are you laughing?'

Stammering, I explained that what she said made it sound like her cat always jumped onto her bed and ejaculated on her face.

Needless to say she wasn't amused and after a couple of stops went by in silence she got off at Clapham Junction telling me she'd forgotten that she'd promised to help her mum with something.

I sometimes see her around town but we don't talk anymore. **– Pete**

Common Error

I went on one date with a guy who lived fairly close to me, and as we were discussing the area I said, 'I live near the common, which is really nice as I like to go jogging.'

The music in the bar was quite loud and he had misheard me.

'So you like to go dogging?'

'No. Jogging.' And so it went on for a while. Actually, quite a while. I think he really wanted to talk about dogging. I think he was quite interested.

I made my excuses and left, keeping as far away from the common as I could. **– Sammy**

Sleepy Head

I arranged to meet up with a guy I'd been messaging on my-singlefriend.com in a bar. I was quite nervous so I was sipping my drink every time there was a lull in the conversation – not realizing I was getting more and more drunk. But the date went really well; I liked the guy, and we decided to move on to a club. There, I left him holding my drink while I nipped to the ladies' – but in my drunken state I passed out in the cubicle, only to be woken some time later by a manager banging on the door, who then escorted me from the club.

They wouldn't let me tell my date I was going, and I didn't have his phone number, so he was left standing at the edge of the dance floor wondering what had happened to me. Despite my emailed apologies the next day, not surprisingly I didn't hear from him again. **– Paula**

Sex Addict

I got chatting to this girl one night as I was walking home. One thing led to another and we went for a drink. We got on like the proverbial house fire, and she ended up coming back to my house. The weirdness came in the early hours as I awoke to damp sheets and her sitting bolt upright, sweating profusely. I asked what was wrong, thinking she had been having a bad dream.

'I must get home,' she said, 'I need my methadone.'

Next time she came round I made sure her bottle was in the fridge. **– Jim**

Crowded Twosome

On a blind date, my date received a text from his friend who was getting married two days later. He informed me that a *few* of his mates were heading this way and they were on a mini stag do. A few, I thought to myself – what, four or five? In come 30 highly inebriated blokes. So the drinking games begin and I am dragged to the next bar. Then the next bar. I enter thinking nothing of it, until I am faced with a number of girls with no clothes on! It dawns on my slow-functioning brain that I am on a blind date with 31 blokes and a load of naked women. My first blind date and the last. **– Jessica**

Texty Beast

I had been chatting to a guy I met through a website and we'd been trying to meet up. Finally, we found a date we could both do, but there was a catch – he was also meeting with two buddies.

On the night, Mr X was clearly not comfortable although his friends were chatty. Despite my best efforts to get a conversation going with him, he seemed uninterested and even started using his mobile while I was mid-sentence. Meanwhile, my phone, which was in my pocket, had been beeping to tell me I had texts...

Not wanting to appear rude, I waited until I went to the loo to read my texts. Imagine my surprise when I saw that they were from Mr X: one saying that any time I wanted to talk I should let him know. Another saying, indignantly, that it was my turn to reply as this was his third message.

I sent a cheeky retort saying that I'd thought it would be rude to check my phone while in company and that any time he wanted to talk I was sitting opposite him. On returning to the table I received another text, and he then called me while I was talking to his friend...

In the next bar, which was underground, I thought I'd try and clear the air with Mr X, and explained I hadn't deliberately ignored his messages, and maybe we should try talking face to face. Incredibly, he got his phone out again. I pointed out the lack of reception but he still insisted on texting me.

At this point I decided enough was enough – I told him that he was an emotional retard and that I was leaving.

Amazingly, he called me a further three times that night asking where I was, why I had left and could he come round. I also heard from him the next morning saying that it had been very nice to meet me – by text, obviously.

Clearly a man in need of serious dating advice. **– Lucy**

Top Trumps

The first person I met from online dating was a guy called Mark. His profile name was Top Trumps which seemed quite sweet and childlike. I met him several times over a few months and we got quite serious about each other. All was going wonderfully well and we decided the time was right for us to sleep together.

It happened, and all was going well until he let out the loudest, longest fart I think I've ever heard. He then let out another, followed by uncontrollable laughter. Then another. This continued, on and on and on, for hours. I think it was three in the morning when he actually stopped farting and laughing and fell asleep.

Needless to say, I never called him. Still, at least I got to find out why he'd called himself Top Trumps. **– Charlie**

Calamity Jane

Being a young minx, I decided to go for a very sexy (but tasteful) pair of thigh boots, some tweed shorts and a black low-cut top on my date. After sushi we went to a bar, ordered drinks and got chatting – about George Bush if memory serves. At this point the booze kicks in, and I can't remember why – or how – but I opened my eyes to find myself straddling this bloke while carrying out a lassoing motion.

I remember looking at what can only be described as the most petrified man I have ever seen, clutching his glass of wine like it was a repellent for Scouse nutjob birds and their lassoes. And that's where the date ended.

Why did I do it? What the hell was I thinking? I have no answers to these questions. All I have is a sinking feeling every time I think about it. **– Suki**

Picture Perfect

Her name was Katy. She was a successful marketing manager. She not only put me at ease, she actually sounded as foxy as her photo too. We arranged to meet.

God, she looked good.

Cocktails, chitchat. First course, chitchat. I'm Scottish and I can tell you, by this time I was roamin' in the haemoglobin.

I excused myself before the main course, looking into the mirror in the gents thinking, 'You lucky bastard.'

I returned to the table and sat down. Then my luck changed.

'I've got something to show you.'

A tattoo, perhaps?

Nope.

Beautiful Katy produced the image I had uploaded to the dating website. My picture. She had downloaded and printed it.

It was laminated.

She then went on to say, 'I've told everyone about us. My Mum says you're a charmer and I've to beware. My Dad isn't too keen on you – but he doesn't even like my husband. Cathy at work thinks Librans and Cancerians just don't make a good couple…'

I'm still searching.

I just ask more questions before I meet internet dates.

– Mark

Killing Time

As a criminal solicitor I regularly come into contact with clients from all walks of life, some of whom ask me out. Obviously, it's never really hard to say no. Criminal *and* a client. Enough said. Not that it's illegal; just not the done thing! However, one caught my eye and we both felt 'the spark', as it were. He had been arrested, the evidence was weak and no further action taken. So no court case; simply an 'innocent' man helping police with their enquiries.

C'mon, I had been single a while at the time. A girl needs a date now and again!

So we met at a pub and I instantly realized that the spark had turned into a damp squib.

Said criminal explained how pleased and honoured he'd been that I accepted. He wanted to start things afresh so suggested he come clean about his past record, bearing in mind that I had obviously had sight of it when dealing with his case. (I had not, as the case went nowhere.) However, I nodded for him to 'fess all.

Hmm. It transpired that said criminal had done some financial irregularities by mistake and spent three years inside for fraud (a small mistake; it was just the judge didn't like him!). His girlfriend at the time saw an opportunity and flogged the house he'd bought with the financial irregularities and cleared off with the proceeds. This piece of news concerned me. Not quite as much as what he said next.

'I then spent the next three years planning her murder.'

He then went into detail about the plot. It involved another criminal who owned a boat, and the plan was to dump his girlfriend into the sea in a barrel. At this point I made my excuses and left.

Needless to say, he was the only criminal I will ever date! But hey, it's a good story! – **Claire**

Language Barrier

Whilst on a business trip in China, our Chinese agent learnt that I was over 40 and not yet married, which, in Chinese culture, is tantamount to having two heads.

Soon, he had arranged for me to have a blind date, and for my date, an insurance clerk, to meet me downstairs in my Shanghai hotel bar. Neutral ground. Safe. Easy getaway for both parties. Fine.

I soon realized that my blind date did not speak much English, but I continued to chat, saying, 'Yes, this is a very strange situation, us meeting like this. You don't know me at all. I could have been a sex fiend or something. Ha ha.'

'What "sex fiend"? she replied. 'You write.'

Heaven knows why, but I wrote it down for her.

'Fiend.' She mouthed the word several times in an attempt to understand its meaning.

'Forget it,' I said, 'It's not important...'

'Fiend?'

'No, it's not important...'

My blind date gets up. She wants to better her English, to understand. She moves to the next table and to the bar staff with the piece of paper, trying to find out what the words mean.

Please, sit down! Forget it!

'Can you tell me what these words mean...?'

I began to shrivel, to shrink. Smaller and smaller...

Blind dates? I'll stick to work thanks. **– Brian**

Name Game

Looking over my card after a speed-dating event (before which I'd had rather a lot of Dutch courage), there were three possible dates: Andy, Matt and Simon. The next day I went online and placed my three ticks in the relevant boxes.

I patiently waited to see if I had any matches. Bingo – I'd got mail. I received an email from Andy asking me for a drink.

The evening came. I walked into the posh London bar and scanned the room but couldn't see the good-looking man I'd chatted to at the speed-dating event. Then, standing before me, was not Andy but Andrew, a rather weathered-looking bald man I'd met at the same event. I sat down, unable to speak, wondering how I was going to pass the evening with a man about 20 years my senior, with whom I had nothing in common, didn't fancy and certainly didn't place a tick next to.

The moral of the story? Ask for a surname. **– Isobel**

Wife Guard

I arranged to meet my date outside a pub. He was late, then all of a sudden there was a man and woman standing in front of me.

The woman said, 'Are you Jackie?'

'Yes.'

'Well, this is Fred and I'm Fred's wife, and I've come to tell you that he's a bastard – a lovable bastard but a bastard nonetheless. This isn't the first time he's done this and it won't be the last...'

Believe it or not, when I got home that night and checked my emails there was one from Fred, saying, 'I'm really sorry about my wife showing up today – I normally delete all my emails but I forgot to delete your last one and she read it and insisted I bring her with me. But you looked really nice so I hope we can get together again very soon, just the two of us.'

Needless to say, we didn't. **– Jackie**

Lighter Side

One dark winter's evening, I had arranged to meet a blind date. It was cold and snowy, so my date said he would collect me. I gave him the address and made sure I was ready so he wouldn't have to knock on the door. Finally, a car pulled up right across the end of the drive. Great, that must be him. I picked up my keys, turned off the lights, shut the door and ran up the drive.

I jumped in looking bright and breezy and smiled.

'Hi, I'm Rachel. It's so nice to meet you!'

He didn't speak. He looked terrified, an unlit cigarette drooping from his lip.

'It's very good of you to collect me. It's such a cold night.'

I fastened my seatbelt and he still said nothing. In fact, he looked more scared than ever. As I settled into the seat and arranged my bag, I finally started to wonder what the problem was.

'You are Simon aren't you...?' I said.

It turned out he'd only pulled over by my house because of the streetlight as he couldn't find his lighter in the car in the dark.

The only thing I could do was reach into my coat pocket, pull out my lighter and light his cigarette... **– Rachel**

Forehead Farewell

My blind date turned out to be a rather large middle-aged lady in jeans and a badly fitting T-shirt.

'So, what's your favourite holiday destination?' she asked. A date is really struggling when the conversation opens with 'So', and it's dead and buried with the first mention of favourite holidays.

As I regaled her with my fascinating Californian trip, my ex turned up with her new boyfriend, the ultimate Gillette Man. Of course, she saw me and made a beeline to my table.

'Hi Paul, how are you? Dave and I have just got back from the Maldives.'

Thanks, but I didn't ask – who gives a shit?

'Aren't you going to introduce me?' she said. For a second

I contemplated introducing my date as a family friend. I could say, 'This is my Auntie Irene.' It wouldn't be that much of a lie because, in truth, she did look like an Auntie Irene. But no, I may be picky and judgmental but I am honest.

'This is Tracey. We're out on a blind date.'

It was as if at that single moment a spotlight was shone on me, and every person in the bar turned to look at me.

After 10 minutes of toe-curling small talk, my ex went on her way to recommence her perfect life with Dave and I was left with Auntie Irene.

'I'll get the bill.'

Dreading the 'goodbye moment' – the kiss, do we meet again? – we made our way to the car park As she puckered up, I leant forwards and kissed her on the forehead. Yes, *the forehead*. To this day I cannot explain why, except perhaps that nobody likes kissing their Auntie... **– Paul**

Burning Desire

My date with Tom was at a party at his house, an international mix of young local professionals, friends and friends of friends. The indoor/outdoor set-up gave it a nice ambience, and the crisp, starry night seemed ideal. Tom ushered us out to the mini-bonfire in the back where we mingled with the crowd.

I made charming conversation with a guest, John, as Tom tended to other guests. Was he avoiding me? I noticed Tom come out onto the deck as I pretended to be absorbed in what John was saying. I leaned close to the fire to keep my back warm, and didn't understand at first why John took a step back and stared down in silent horror at my right leg. I followed his eyes downwards, just as I felt hot flames searing the skin on my calf above my boot. Instinctively, I kicked at the flame with my left foot, lighting my other jean leg and causing panic among the party guests as I hopped and kicked madly in the middle of the crowd. Finally, John reacted and poured his beer on my right leg. A stranger on my right did the same and the flames were extinguished on both sides.

My boots were burnt from beige to black, and my new jeans were in black tatters up to the knees and beer-soaked, but Tom invited me to his room to clean up my burns, and the rest of the night was great. **– Shelby**

Lez Be Friends

After a five-minute first date in the pub and a bizarre finger-sucking second in the cinema, my third date with 26-year-old Mandy was in Leicester Square. As she lived in London and I did not, I wondered whether this might be my chance to go back to hers for coffee. Or better still, 'coffee'.

We were inside a restaurant offering faux-Mexican fare, sipping on margaritas, when she said my name and then paused. Over the years I've learnt that this is usually a prelude to extraordinarily bad news.

'I'm already seeing someone,' said Mandy. 'Actually, I'm living with them.'

'I thought you said you didn't have a boyfriend?'

'I don't. I'm living with a woman. But I'd like to keep seeing you if you're all right with that.'

And be in with a chance of a three-in-a-bed romp with a couple of lesbians? 'Fine by me.'

I never did get the threesome, though. **– Jamie**

School Daze

Rewind about 15 years to my school days in a town in Kent, where a young man called Mel was popular amongst the female fraternity, and I too found myself lusting after him. He was one of those sporty, fresh-faced, all round 'good' guys who seemed like very good boyfriend material.

Moving on 13 years, a friend of mine had got back in touch with him. She made a point of telling me he was on the market, looking for a nice girl and that as we both liked cycling perhaps we should go out. Could it be fate?

The date started badly. He had made no effort to dress up. He didn't offer to get me a drink and he told me that I reminded him of Bridget Jones.

When I returned from the toilet he was on his mobile to his

brother, a chat I had to sit through, like a spare part, for 15 minutes. I was absolutely dying to go, but as it hadn't quite reached 8.30pm I thought it would be rude to make my excuses any earlier than 9pm.

No need. He got there first. *He* got there first! The biggest insult of my life.

I got home to my housemates, burst into tears, had a glass of wine and then gradually, very gradually, started to see the funny side. It's a very big word of warning, though, that those childhood sweethearts don't always grow into the lovely, interesting, handsome potential boyfriends you'd like them to! **– Briony**

Mandy Advice

Despite my initial reservations about internet dating I decided to throw myself in at the deep end. After all, the guy was cute, he was a trainee doctor and, to be honest, I was getting desperate by this stage. My date was with Aiden, at a house party. After two hours of awkward conversation (how was I supposed to know that everybody in the room was in the university jazz ensemble?) Aiden suggested we go to his room, an offer I gladly accepted.

'Are you okay in there, Aiden?' I shouted in the direction of the en-suite – he'd been in there for 20 minutes already. As he strutted out and announced I should now be referring to him as Amanda, I decided it was time to leave.

My second date was a little more successful. James and John has a certain ring, don't you think? **– John**

Great Catch

I suggested we meet in York for lunch. I left my friends in the city and promised to meet them a couple of hours later at the Minster. I arrived at the station and there was the man I was about to spend two hours with. He was what I'd call averagely ugly, with bottle-top glasses, too-short trousers and slip-on grey shoes.

On speaking to him, I knew he really wasn't for me at all, but I figured that at least we'd have a nice lunch.

'Let me take you to a favourite haunt of mine,' he said. 'Somewhere I frequented in my younger days.'

As we walked in my heart sank. His favourite haunt was my idea of a nightmare. Swirly carpet, heavy smoke, fruit machines on every wall and half a dozen 50-something shotaway men on bar stools gazing into pints.

A Diet Coke and a nasty prawn bap later, I said it was about time I left as I had to meet my friends. We split the bill – to the last penny.

As we walked up the road I felt I had to say it was nice to meet him. Then, to change the subject, I casually said, 'I'm meeting my friends at the Minster. You could come along...'

To which he replied, 'Ah, I see – you want to show me off to your friends now.' **– Pam**

Bad Trip

Years ago, I was so pleased when a bloke I'd fancied for ages asked me out. Since we both liked live music we arranged to meet at a pub that was putting on a local band. When I arrived, the first thing my date told me was that he'd just taken acid. Needless to say, we didn't see each other again.
   – Carla

Tongue Tied

On a date I laughed politely at something he had said, and he stopped me and put his hand on mine, saying, 'I have to tell you this.' I waited a little anxiously. 'You have the cleanest tongue I have ever seen.'
   I looked at him a bit lost for words.
   He proceeded with, 'So tell me. Do you clean it?'
   I don't think I have ever been so happy to finish a date.
   – Alison

Fast Worker

On our first meeting, my date asked if we could raise our kids Catholic, which took me by some surprise. I tried to ignore it, but there it was hanging in the air like a bad smell. Our kids? Perhaps I'm not up with the times and maybe it's an entirely appropriate question to ask someone after knowing them for three hours, but planning the next 10 years seemed a little premature... **– Jenny**

Sick Story

I am a hairdresser, and had a client who had been coming into the salon for about three years. He was gorgeous: a confident, successful businessman, very wealthy and drove a Ferrari. He had asked me out numerous times but the timing was never right. This one time he asked me out, I said yes, and we arranged to meet at a lovely restaurant.

On arrival, I thought he was acting strangely but put it down to nerves. He had a bottle of champagne at the table; the waiter poured us a glass then took it away because it was empty, returning with another which my date drank, very quickly.

Another bottle appeared.

By this time he was plastered, and when I suggested he might slow down he ignored me, said he was fine and carried on drinking. I kept pouring him glasses of water but he knocked them over three times and the waiters had to come and clean up.

Returning from the loo, he shouted for another bottle. The manager came across and told him that they couldn't serve him any more, and could he keep the noise down as he was disturbing the other diners.

At this point, he very noisily burst into tears, shouting that they had ruined his first date with the only girl he had ever loved. I was mortified and tried to calm him down but he was sobbing. I asked the waiters to bring us some coffee and water, and tried to reassure him that the night wasn't ruined (well, I couldn't upset him any more – and he had snot hanging off his nose at this point). He eventually calmed down enough to drink the coffee, but then all of a sudden went white, stood up, vomited all over the place and passed out in the middle of the restaurant. Suffice to say, I'd had enough, got my coat and left, with all the waiters fussing round him.

Funnily enough, he never came to the salon again.

– Becky

Chapter Seventeen

'You're Gonna Love My Mates'

and now the screaming starts

If your new partner appears to have no friends, then there's something up. It's known as the, 'Hmm, nobody likes to hang out with my new partner – I wonder if I'm about to find out why…' dilemma. If they have just two friends, one of whom is Nigel, an 'online friend', and the other is their mum then, sorry, but you've actually got a problem – a similar predicament to the no-friends issue, in fact, except with bandwidth and Oedipal complications thrown in for good measure.

If, on the other hand, they've got a wide and varied social circle made up of work colleagues, old school pals and even the odd ex or two that they've stayed in touch with, then congratulations – you probably won't be spending Saturday afternoons shopping for their mum. But guess what?

You've *still* got a problem.

Because this is a group of people who, combined, know pretty much all there is to know about the gory details of your partner's past. They may even be the gory details of your partner's past. They know what your new flame got up to at school, exactly what happened at Alex's party in 1997, why your partner can't stomach smoky bacon crisps and much – so much – more. They know all the good stuff. But they also know all the dark stuff.

So, let's not pretend that meeting these people is going to be a breeze. It's not. It's about the only time in your life when you get to meet a whole new group of people and be interviewed at the same time. 'It's not a test,' you'll tell yourself. Well, sorry, but it *is* a test. Not only that, but after the first date it's probably the single most important social occasion of your relationship. Still, remember this: your new partner likes you and wants you to be part of their gang, so you've got a bit of a head start.

Friends or Foes?

With any luck your new beau will introduce you to their friends in small doses – one or maybe two pals at a time. Expect to see one or more of this lot on your travels…

Bad-influence Friends

You won't necessarily recognize this friend-type from the outset because the first time you meet them they'll be nice as pie: the smiling, warm-welcome, life-and-soul of the new-partner party.

Next thing you know they're luring your other half to strip joints. Or getting them legless before boarding a ferry to France. Clearly this is going to grind. You'd have to be Saint Doormat not to be a tad alarmed by this kind of behaviour. But why? Are you concerned for health and safety issues – that your partner's going to fall off the ferry clutching a bottle of Smirnoff? Or is it really that you're scared they're going on the pull with their bad-influence buddy?

If it's the latter (which it is, isn't it? Be honest…) then you have to deal with some trust issues. Share your concerns with your partner. If they admit to joining their friend on the pull (wait for the hoary old chestnut: 'but I didn't do anything') then you've got every right not to be happy, whatever they say. If they don't really care that this upsets you, you might want to think seriously about whether you can live with the scenario. Most of us can't, and certainly, we are all worth more than that.

If it's their safety you're concerned about, then that's a different ball-game. Maybe they enjoy the thrill of this danger-ous and exciting person? Is that threatening to you? Frustrat-ing though it is, you will have to wait for your partner to realize

that this friendship is a demanding and potentially danger-
ous one for them – before the trip to A&E.

Female bad-influence friends
are often (but not always) called: Nikki,
Lucy or Bex.

Male bad-influence friends are
often (but not always) called: Snorter,
Si or Jim-Bob.

The Jealous Friend

Please save us from the jealous friend! A person so pathet-
ically insecure that they seem to be making it their life's work
to split you and your partner up. They will try to do it with
jokes and insinuations. They will bring up stories from your
partner's (often sexual) past then – oops! – pretend they forgot themselves. They will endeavour to share private jokes.
Everything they talk about will have happened 'before you
two got together'. They must be educated. Or terminated.

You may wish you had access to a bloke called Terry, a bag
of lime, a spade and a cold October night, but it's only this
behaviour that must be terminated. And one of the ways you
can do this is to kill it with kindness. Remember, any aggres-
sive behaviour on Jealous Friend's behalf is because they're
weak, pathetic, lonely and lily-livered. In short, they feel threatened, the poor lamb. Their weapon is spite. They expect you
to deploy it in return. Don't give them the satisfaction.

Jealous Friend A

- **What they do:** All of a sudden Jealous Friend A 'needs' your partner. They 'really need' your partner 'right now' because... their whites aren't white enough, or their dog gave them a funny look – or they are just feeling 'a bit sad' or something equally nose-wipey.

- **What you do:** You absolutely must not respond by getting clingy. Jealous Friend A is already winning hands down when it comes to needy and flaky behaviour. It's a contest you cannot – and indeed do not want to – win (after all, your partner isn't sharing bedroom antics with the jealous friend – you hope). Go with the flow until the penny drops and your other half realizes how fabulously light-hearted you are in comparison, and how consoling Jealous Friend A is actually just a pain in the arse, at which point you have won. Game over.

Jealous Friend B

- **What they do:** Jealous Friend B regales you with anecdotes involving your partner's past. You feel uncomfortable. These supposedly 'hilarious' tales are in fact designed specifically to make you feel excluded and uncomfortable. They're killers with smiles, Jealous Friends, they really are.

- **What you do:** Get in there. Ask more about this situation. Show interest in whatever they have to say, and slowly – like a particularly dim-witted dog – they will learn that this tactic isn't going to lose you sleep at night. Plus, of course, you've been using your time profitably by charming your partner's other pals, who are now beginning to agree en masse that Jealous Friend B is acting like a total arse. Jealous Friend B now has two options: 1) leaving the group and abandoning their car at Beachy Head, or 2) starting afresh with you. Either option's cool, yes? Game over.

However tough you think you are, however witty and spiky you can be, don't attempt to lock horns with this succubus. Trust us on this one. Why? First, because it's their game, only they know all the rules and they've hidden the dice. Second, you don't want your new crush to spend any time counselling either side about how you both feel. And remember, it is likely that the one who has been hanging around the longest (i.e. not you) will get the interested ear of your partner. Third, once your partner has been informed that there is a situation, a problem has been added to your relationship. Don't let that happen as it's really not your problem, and you don't want it sitting at the dinner table with you and your loved one. If asked, lie and claim you think they are delightful. End of conversation.

Female jealous friends are often (but not always) called: Fi, Jo or Eleanor

Male jealous friends are often (but not always) called: Karl, Spencer or Mark

The Ex (Ugh)

It's a fact of life (hell, it's probably even the law) that your partner won't tell you about an ex until *after* you've met the person in question. Even then the history will be underplayed in such vague and casual terms that you'll be left wondering if they did actually shag, or just bumped into each other once in Tesco on a Wednesday afternoon. Face it, you'll never get the whole truth out of them, and nor should you try unless you want to come across as clingy and paranoid. Just remember that there's a difference between what they say and what they mean (and bear in mind you're doing it yourself). They are not being shifty; they are ashamed – let it be.

What They Say

'I guess there was an attraction. Once. Years ago. Kind of. But that's as far as it went really.'

What They Mean

'We snogged once, and ever since there has been a perpetual, bittersweet sense of what-might-have-been that seems to crackle and pop in the air around us whenever we meet.'

What They Say	**What They Mean**
'Well, I think we might have kissed once – at a party or something. Bit pissed. To be honest, I can't really remember.'	'Yes, one lonely, rainy night we did indeed find comfort in each other's arms. I shall never forget it. There is a perpetual, bittersweet sense, blah blah blah...'
'We did have a night together once. We were rubbish at it. It was pretty embarrassing and awful if I'm honest. Nothing in it at all, God forbid.'	'We were at it like rabbits on Viagra for months. I still fantasize remembering our luvving and there is a perpetual, bittersweet sense, blah blah blah...'

If all that sounds difficult to chew on, just remember that you're telling these whoppers yourself. 'It was just a peck on the cheek,' you'll innocently claim, recalling that knee trembler in the cubicles at Laura's wedding. Knowing it's there but not getting hung up on it is one of the dark arts of relationships. Used correctly, the unmentionable dark stuff is what gives your relationship its frisson. You have no option but to lie as this is the only way you can maintain that this fresh new relationship is the one for you – after all, they have to be better in all ways, or you are just cruel.

Once you've negotiated the long, tortuous, vague and

elliptical route to establishing that, yes, okay, if we're honest, the person you've just met did indeed get slurpy with your new partner, your natural reaction will be to reach for the knife drawer. However, to paraphrase Monty Python, always look on the bright side of an ex in their life, and consider this:

They didn't kill their ex. Neither – and hopefully you can visually corroborate this – has there been any history of disfiguring violence in their relationship. You're already ahead on points here.

Despite the history, their ex still thinks they are a good egg. After all they've no doubt been through together, this pair is still on speaking terms. Yay!

The group accepts exes. Yay and double yay!

'Ah, but,' says Captain Paranoia perched on your shoulder, 'what if Ex Number One is knocking around in the hope of adding a little extra Fahrenheit to that old flame?'

It's a possibility, sure – one you'd have to be deluded to dismiss. But on the other hand, just because you think your new toy is the hottest thing since the last volcanic era, with the looks of Apollo and the nature of Bobby Ewing, that doesn't necessarily mean the ex wants them back. Newsflash: they broke up!

Sure, it's natural to feel anxiety over this one. Chances are your partner and their ex will also be feeling a bit weird about it. So talk. Don't make a real-life, breaking-news issue over the situation as it's simply not their fault that this is a bit awkward for you. Don't compete with or compare yourself to the ex because – this just in – they broke up! And don't be threatened that there is someone in the group who has shared bedroom wonders with your partner... they broke up!

Female exes are usually (but not always) called: Janey, Claire or Kerry

Male exes are usually (but not always) called: Tom, Sam or Jon

FAQs (Friend Angst Queries)

How Should I Act with My New Partner around Their Friends?

The worst thing you can do is to be clingy around your new partner. They want to see how you fit in, not have to look after you. However, if they abandon you, do not introduce you, leave you for 40 days and nights in a desert of new faces, think very hard about whether to book your next date. If you can't cope with that, it's unlikely to change.

How Should I Act with Their Friends?

Be yourself, it's all you've got. Remember all that stuff about listening and asking questions? Use it here. You can only listen if you ask questions/integrate yourself. A lot of people like to share their details of their lives, so ask about them. Not about how many valves their Vauxhall Nova has, but, for example, what they do for a living. Do they like it? That's a great start. Remember to actually listen to the reply, though!

I Haven't Been Introduced to Their Friends Yet? What's Up?

The wormy-worm of paranoia says they're embarrassed to be seen with you, yes? Maybe not. It might simply be that they are still working out whether you are right for them. Any stay of execution can go massively in your favour, too, so don't be pushy. However, if you have been dating for months on end, and still no pals, there's something up. Get to the bottom of it.

Frankly, We're Way too Loved-up to Bother Meeting Mates. That's Okay, Isn't It?

Nope! After your initial months of steaming up the bedroom windows you simply have to emerge one day. Just because you're feeling snug on the sofa, happy with the thought of staring into each other's eyes until the second coming, the bad news is that one evening, while pressing play on the DVD player, you are likely to feel a trifle bored. Keep the friends on board, you need them. They make you laugh, listen to you when you cry, and usually have a spare tenner when you need it.

Help! My New Partner's Best Friend Made a Pass at Me!

Like sharing a bath with your mum, this is best avoided and awkward when it happens. There are two lanes to go down: snog them back or rebuff them. If you went for it, well, boy, are you in turmoil now. You need to decide who you want to be with now, and quick. Once you have made that decision there will be body parts to pick up. Tough. You did it, you mop it.

If you rebuffed them, you've got to hope they will be feeling like a proper pillock. If not, they are not a good friend to your partner. Only in this scenario should you hallucinate about revealing the incident.

Oh yes – should you tell your partner? Answer, only if the pest keeps pestering, or if you're a chaos junkie. Otherwise, keep schtum. If you do decide to tell (and the only reason for doing so should be the fear of the pest getting in there first and claiming you started it) then play it down as much as possible.

Finally, don't be too scared about meeting this group of people. They are a 'safe place' for your partner. They know your partner; they care about your partner. Your partner probably thinks they are funny, and for that reason enjoys spending time with them. If you aren't wearing rose-tinted specs while looking at your new boy/girlfriend then you will undoubtedly like most of their friends.

Chapter Eighteen

'The Folks Are Dying to Meet You'

time to face your parent paranoia

To say that meeting your new partner's family is a bit of a mine-field is, of course, getting things ridiculously out of proportion.

No, it's *far* more frightening than that. Sure, mines may take off a leg, but they can't destroy your soul. Mines won't sit at the head of the dinner table seething with silent resentment at your very presence, nor will they throw a wobbly if you forget to take your shoes off at the front door. And unless you're in the habit of pulling at Middle Eastern arms fairs, you'll never have to compete with a mine for your partner's attention. No, mines are a doddle in comparison to meeting the other half's parents.

So, what can you expect? Extensive scientific research has revealed that there are three types of parent: the consultant, the helicopter and the drill sergeant. Rubbish! Our research (that is, we asked our friends) has gone one better and found four. Here they are, and how to deal with them...

1. The Society Parents

- **Also known as:** Mummy and Daddy, Ma and Pa, 'the rentals'.

- **Distinguishing marks:** They live in a really big house, which may be a bit draughty. If you're 12 it's great fun to run around; if you're in your mid-20s you might get yourself lost in the middle of the night while trying to find the loo.

- **Clothes:** Society parents are not necessarily rich. That's why they can't afford cardies without holes in them. Corduroy is worn. Very worn. Wellington boots are green but covered with mud.

- **Pets:** Yes, trillions. Society people love their animals more than life itself.

- **Holidays:** Don't be *ridiculous*.

- **Food:** Grouse. The source of that appalling smell you thought was a dead animal rotting beneath the floorboards is in fact about to be served to you. Yum.

- **How to survive them:** Your best attack here is surprise – be inventive, artistic, a little strange, wear pink stilettos. They won't know who you are, but Mummy at least will think you are rather unconventional, and that's just 'super'. A small shock here and there to exhibit your boho nature will pay dividends (like saying 'fuck' at supper), and they'll end up asking who your parents are. Do not answer, 'Mrs and Mrs Neck from Aldershot,' as that's not what they mean. It's best to sigh, 'I really don't know anymore,' or even better: 'An Argentinian artist…' (they'll think polo) '…and his teenage muse' (they'll think 'just like Daddy').

    Bamboozle them with short, sharp exoticisms and they'll adore you. Bear in mind there is no family stranger than an aristocratic one, and invariably their own history includes affairs, fraud, slavery, depravity, poverty, immense wealth, missing children and murder. They love it. Don't ever let on that you don't know what they are talking about, and never fill your boots on the second course, as they may surprise you with several more. Do not look surprised; in fact, practise 'no surprise' with this kind of clan, especially when they get very, very drunk and start making passes at you. Needless to say, this lot are great fun.

- **Must always:** send a stiff thank-you card after each and every visit.

- **Must never:** use your fork as a shovel.

2. The 'Second-marriage' Parents

- **Also known as:** Mum and Dad.

- **Distinguishing marks:** When you pull up to their respectable but unassuming detached home in St Albans, second-marriage parents will be standing on the doorstep to greet you, holding hands. They will demur when you offer to remove your shoes (but really they'd like you to do so) and usher you inside, neatly hanging your coat on a hook by the front door, beside which there will be a photograph of your partner with their ex, taken during a family holiday.

  Despite the fact that they 'really did rather like' the ex, they're going to make the effort with you, especially Dad, who isn't your partner's real dad, even though he likes your partner to call him dad, 'because dad's a state of mind, too'. So Dad will ask you about the journey. If you're a boy, he'll expect you to know which services on the A1 are currently closed for refurbishment and how many miles to the gallon your Peugeot does. If you're a girl, he'll offer to check your oil and tyre pressure for you, beaming happily when you accept, nipping upstairs to put on some old trousers and returning in a pair that look identical to those he had on. 'Oh, those tatty things,' second-marriage Mum will gently chide, before sharing some tips on gravy or, if you're a boy, offering you a small lager.

Their house will be frighteningly tidy, a cat will be asleep on the sofa, and copies of the *Daily Mail* will be folded and placed in a magazine rack. They'll tell you that Dad once wrote a funny letter to Terry Wogan, although it was never read out on air.

- **Clothes:** Like everything else, their wardrobe will be neat, tidy, unassuming and paid-for.

- **Pets:** A cat beloved by Mum that Dad pretends to hate, but doesn't really, the card.

- **Holidays:** Dorset in the caravan and two weeks in France every year. 'It's a lovely country,' Dad will say. 'Wasted on the bloody French, of course.'

- **Food:** A Sunday roast that Delia would be proud of, prepared by Mum and carved by Dad – who always performs this task with a tea towel draped over one shoulder.

- **How to survive them:** Second-marriage parents have been burnt in love themselves, and what's great now is that they've found happiness a second time around. But with new love comes new vanity. So you should be aware that all they really want to see across the dinner table is a mirror reflecting slightly younger versions of themselves. Generally speaking, they will take as they find and, as they've been around the block a bit themselves, they're likely to be very tolerant of whatever little foibles you might have.

- **Must always:** laugh at Dad's jokes.

- **Must never:** be anything but polite and unassuming.

3. The Bling Parents

- **Also known as:** MUM! DAD!

- **Distinguishing marks:** Whether it's a mock-Georgian house in Surrey with a BMW on the drive or a council flat in Croydon, the bling parents will be heard before they're seen. Arriving, you'll find Dad in front of Sky on the widescreen, volume high, with a can of Foster's close at hand, shouting for Mum, who is in the kitchen trying to make something from a Jamie Oliver cookbook, while simultaneously watching the *EastEnders* omnibus, listening to 'Angels' by Robbie Williams, smoking a Peter Stuyvesant and chewing gum.

Reluctant to grow old, and bewilderingly over-sexed, Mum has recently had a tattoo on her shoulder, and is considering a nipple piercing, while Dad is squeezed into Nike and sometimes reads *Heat* on the toilet. Whatever the vintage of your partner, there will be a sibling aged about five who, if a boy, will have a shaved head and an ASBO, and if a girl will be wearing make-up, a pair of her mother's high heels and a T-shirt saying 'Porn Star'.

- **Clothes:** Mum wears strappy tops to show off her 'charms'; Dad bulges out of something sporty that doesn't require a belt.

- **Pets:** Tyson was put down after that nasty business over at the kiddies' playground.

- **Food:** A barbie with Dad cooking (sporting regulation novelty 'nude' apron); Mum by the pool wearing see-through high heels.

- **Holidays:** Magaluf until recently, but they've since taken up golf and can now be heard breaching the peace on Mediterranean golf courses before going for 'a bop' in the resort nightclub.

- **How to survive them:** As with all parent types, their bark is worse than their bite. Remember, these people *want* to like you. Their offspring likes you, so you're already ahead on points. Plus, bling Mum and Dad pride themselves on still being 'young', so relax, treat the place as your own, make a few off-colour jokes, feign interest in football and celebrity gossip. Careful not to get too friendly, though. This parent-type will want invitations to hen parties/stag nights and so on, and they'll get very drunk and shout a lot.

- **Must always:** support England.

- **Must never:** beat Dad at PlayStation.

4. The *Guardian-* reading Parents

- **Also known as:** Vicky and Keith.

- **Distinguishing marks:** 'Call me Keith,' Dad will say, once you've made the short walk from Highbury and Islington tube to their flat, which, he claims, was bought before the boom. Vicky will wipe her hands on an apron made from free-range hemp before giving you a welcome mwah-mwah kiss (on *both* cheeks), and offering you a glass of something organic bought yesterday from a farmers' market off Marylebone High Street.

The flat has wooden flooring throughout and is decorated mainly with bookshelves and photographs of Vicky and Keith taken at Glastonbury in 1978, 'before it went commercial'. Phallic sculptures, idols and other souvenirs of trips to Third World countries will adorn the windowsills, while invitations to viewings and letters from charities will sit on the mantelpiece. In the fridge is hummus, Budvar and blueberries (all of which are Fair Trade). The conversation includes phrases like 'do you know where I'm coming from?' and constant allusions to their 'colourful past' that you suspect goes only as far as trying to smoke banana skins in the early 1970s.

- **Clothes:** Mum wears stripes, bought from Jigsaw; Dad wears tight T-shirts from Slam City Skates.

- **Pets:** Snoopy, a terrier rescued from an animal shelter in 1984. Blind in one eye and incontinent.

- **Holidays:** They have a place in the Cotswolds and make a great show of being disappointed that the 'Primrose Hill set' have started colonizing the place (although secretly they loved it when they saw Kate Moss in Stow-on-the-Wold).

- **Food:** The *Guardian*-reading parents only eat 'adjective food': free-range meat, organic milk, low-cholesterol hummus, cruelty-free coffee. Adjective food is purchased from health-food shops and farmers' markets, even though Vicky once fainted when she saw a live chicken.

- **How to survive them:** Go with the flow – they do. You can have a great time visiting *Guardian*-reading parents since it would go against everything they believe in to be at all judgmental. Ever fancied reinventing yourself as a mad, poetry-writing free spirit? Now's your chance!

- **Must always:** remember their birthdays.

- **Must never:** mention Margaret Thatcher.

So, the watchword is similar to meeting your new partner's friends – be yourself – only with the caveat here that you mould yourself to the surroundings. You're meeting these people on their home turf, so they'll already be sending out strong messages as to how they expect to be treated. The trick is to read those messages and respond to them. Get it right and your partner will be so grateful you won't walk properly for a week. Get it wrong? Ker-boom.

Chapter Nineteen

'I Think This Is the One'

from perfect catch to perfect match

It's five dates down the line and you've started saying 'we' instead of 'I'. But before you go breaking out the L-word or booking the church, check that you're not being blinded by new-date bliss. Have a look at the character types described below, and the sort of partner who would suit them. Bear in mind that these profiles are exaggerated – anybody who actually suited one of these types to the letter would be a right nutter – but they're a useful yardstick to help you work out if your new pal is right for you or a right old handful.

Drama Queens and Crisis Kings

This is the kind of person for whom a quiet life and content-ment are the sexual equivalent of dirty washing-up water – boring, dull and grey, and to be avoided at all costs.

They thrive on drama, but unfortunately not the kind you can see at the theatre. There's no such thing as a quiet and considered chat on the sofa with this type of person. It's fly-ing crockery, fist-fights with angry neighbours, insults and recriminations. For them it's all about grand, screeching break-ups followed by exhausting, noisy make-ups. They dress to kill, even if it's just a trip to the corner shop. They fly off the handle at the slightest thing and analyse even the most innocent of comments for perceived insults. Such as...

'Hi, there.'

'High? *High?* Are you saying I'm on drugs? Great – once a junkie always a junkie, is it? Give a dog a bad name...' (Need-less to say they will have some kind of history of addiction to *something*, be it heroin, sex or just chucking plates at anyone unfortunate enough to be in the vicinity.)

In short, they are a *nightmare*, and life with them is a roller coaster, but sadly not the nice sort that Ronan Keating sings about. No, on this particular ride, you've just heard a strange clanking sound, a school kid in front of you has thrown up and you really, really want to get off – but can't because you're strapped in.

On the other hand…   Life is never, ever dull with this kind of partner, and there's a lot to be said for that. Plus, the sex is always great (and there's a lot to be said for that, too).

Perfect match   A drama queen and crisis king together are simply a break-up waiting to happen. Either they'll kill each other, the courts will ban them from seeing each other, or one of them will decide they need fresh meat and leave – a decision that will, of course, provoke even more ferocious arguments and possible bloodshed. Which is *great* for the drama queen and crisis king.

In fact, the ideal partner for the drama queen or crisis king is somebody who is monumentally laid-back, so chilled-out they're barely sentient. Preferably, they'll also be also skilled in a martial art and have sharp reflexes for catching all that flying crockery.

But even for the chilled-out partner, the chaos junkie is a novelty that wears off very, very quickly indeed.

The Siamese Twin

Once you're with a Siamese twin, that's it. You're on permanent call, night and day, 24/7. Your weekends are no longer your own, and neither will you be allowed any privacy or secrecy. They will want to know where you were today, with whom and for how long. Equally, they will want to know what you plan to do tomorrow, where, with whom and for how long.

This person considers it perfectly normal to read your diary, journal or private letters. Any objection to them doing this will be considered an admission of either infidelity or unreciprocated love. You will be expected to provide unlimited attention at all times, as well as constant gifts in order to 'prove' your undying love.

On the other hand... This person will be the most loving, caring and attentive partner you could possibly hope for, and will shower you with unending affection. Aw...

The perfect match A protective partner is perfect for the Siamese twin – someone who will not only put up with the never-ending love-storm, but encourage and positively revel in it too. For the female Siamese twin, this is the proverbial big, strong man; and a nurturing mother-figure is right for the male Siamese twin. Of course, this kind of obsessive neediness can get wearing, but if both partners understand the deal and know when to play up to it and when to pull away, there's no reason why this kind of match shouldn't be a goody.

The Free Spirit

For this kind of person a relationship is important, but it's not the be-all and end-all of their life. They'll have friends you rarely meet, and interests and activities or work commitments that take them away from you – maybe for long periods at a time. If you ask about these friends or activities you will be met either with frustratingly ambiguous answers or accusations that you're snooping. An innocent enquiry about their day will be interpreted as suffocating and needy. They hardly ever have their mobile switched on and get annoyed if you ring it when they do. They will turn up at odd times of the day with vague explanations for their lateness. They will frustrate the hell out of you.

On the other hand… This sort of person tends to compartmentalize their life, moving from box to box. But doing this allows them to give each area of their life their undivided attention and enthusiasm. You're one of those boxes, so when you have the free spirit all to yourself, you have the best of them: attentive, loving and passionate.

The perfect match Another free spirit is the best kind of match here, a partner who's not seeking Siamese togetherness but knows the importance of top-quality time together. Still, it's the kind of match-up that needs work from both parties, since there's a tendency for each of you to become complacent. Providing that doesn't happen – and you make sure you set aside (yuck alert) 'special time' for the relationship – this partnership should pass its medical with flying colours.

Compatibility Stumbling Blocks

Anyone sound familiar? Perhaps not at this stage. After all, the key to any new fling is flexibility and compromise. Plus, your new partner will have been on their very best behaviour up to now. Inevitably, this means the early stages of romance are spent working out exactly who this is who's lighting your fire all of a sudden.

What's make-or-break and what isn't will be up to you to decide, but here are some of the most common compatibility stumbling blocks, and how to find out whether or not you and your new beau are on the same wavelength – or about to wave bye-bye.

Interests

It's not going to make or break the relationship if you don't have interests in common, and in fact it's the kind of thing that becomes less important as time goes on. Even so, common interests do help...

- **How do you go there?** This is the kind of thing you're going to cover on your first few dates. Remember that early-date best-behaviour rule, though: people tend to invent interests they don't really have, especially if they think there's a shag at the end of it.

Career

It's an ambition thing, really. There's nothing worse than one partner who's happy to count paperclips until they're 65, while the other wants to shimmy up the corporate ladder. Hardly the kind of thing you should be broaching on date three, though...

- **How do you go there?** Don't ask, 'What are your goals?' That's creepy and rude. But a few conversations about work and money should give you a general impression of their financial aspirations. Are they generous with their money? A philanthropist and charity-giver, or a right tight-arse? Steer them past a *Big Issue* seller and see how they react if this is important to you.

Sex

It's a fact of life (and not a *sad* fact, necessarily, just a fact) that the only way you can tell whether or not you're sexually compatible with your partner is to have sex with them. It's a dirty job, etc...

- **How do you go there?** Well, shagging is pretty much the only way. However, unless you're the world's least intuitive thicko, you should get an idea of your new buddy's sexual appetite just from chatting to them. How do they react when the subject comes up in conversation, for example? Or when you're leafing through the latest sex-obsessed celeb mag together?

Travel

Some people are homebodies; others have a well-thumbed passport and the tales to go with it. The urge to see the world can be a hugely determining factor in your compatibility. After all, what are you going to do when one of you wants to spend three weeks in India while the other one's quite happy with a long weekend in Skegness?

- **How do you go there?** Let's face it – it's going to come up before you're that far into your relationship. However, the travel-shy are notorious for keeping their lack of frontier spirit under wraps, so don't necessarily take their word for it. 'I like travel' could mean they're happy with a week in Majorca and some souvenir sunburn, whereas you're not satisfied unless you've scaled a major mountain range. Try and squeeze some travel anecdotes out of them – shouldn't be too hard if they really do like heading for the sunset. In fact, you probably won't be able to shut them up. If, on the other hand, they lead off with, 'Uh, yeah, Cambodia was quite, uh, hot,' then the little alarm bells should probably be ringing…

Marriage

Depending on how old you are, this is an issue that's going to come up sooner or later. Some people love the idea of marriage; whereas to others it's like suggesting a frontal lobotomy – minus anaesthetic.

- **How do you go there?** Men don't like talking about marriage. Actually, men would sooner stick fish-hooks into their eyes than talk about marriage, especially at the beginning of a relationship. Bring it up at any time within the first six months of your romance and he'll be excusing himself for the loo – then seeing if he can fit through the window to escape.

  Equally, if you're a man, then talking about marriage will start the klaxons going in her head because men just aren't supposed to be interested in that sort of stuff.

  So, if it's on your agenda and you want to know if it features in your new partner's life plans, what do you do? The best approach is to talk about a mate's wedding or impending nuptials, doing so in purely anecdotal terms. How they respond to the conversation should give you an idea of their views on the subject. Better yet, see if you can drag them along to a friend's wedding. Are they sitting there dewy-eyed, or with a permanent Sid Vicious-style sneer?

Kids

And you thought marriage was the biggie. Again (and once again it depends on your age), children could be high on your list of partner-priorities, and it stands to reason that you want to know how your new best buddy feels about the pitter-patter of tiny jailers' feet. If you definitely want them and your partner definitely doesn't then, mercenary as it sounds, you may be wasting your precious libido.

And please don't make the mistake of hanging on thinking you're going to persuade them either way – you probably won't. Most people will not admit to wanting children if they are asked directly so, again, be subtle. Talk about the subject through a third party, or perhaps ask your partner about their childhood first and then ask if they would want the same sort of thing for their children.

- **How do you get there?** Once again, this is not a subject that should be broached in the first flush of romance. But the two of you are seeing a lot of each other, yes? You're gazing into each other's eyes over dinner and going on long afternoon walks. At some point the subject of those small people who run around school playgrounds is going to come up. Rather than weigh in with, 'So, do you want children then, or what?' use your natural instinct and cunning to judge how they feel about the little blighters. With this subject, as with marriage, people will often use any opportunity they can to make their feelings clear. Just like you, they want to get their opinions out in the open without damaging the great thing you've got going on.

Just remember that this relationship stuff is never an exact science, and at the end of the day you'll always need to rely on the most important skill you've got – your instinct.

Chapter Twenty

Step Out the Back, Jack

almost 50 ways to dump or get dumped

It's a fact of life that relationships go one of three ways:

- The two of you sitting in front of *The X-Factor* on a Saturday night with an empty carton of Häagen-Dazs between you, picking fluff out of each other's belly buttons.
- One of you getting dumped.
- The police searching for recently disturbed earth on the outskirts of Epping Forest.

So, when you look at it like that, being dumped is actually the *second best* thing that could happen to any relationship. If you can't stick the sight of pop wannabes, it may even go straight in at number one.

Even so, it's never nice, especially if you're on the receiving end. All you can do is hope that your partner will be honest and grown-up about it. Like you would be, of course, if you were the one doing the dumping…

Am I Being Dumped? Me, Who's Given so Much?

You know that moment in a relationship when it's all been motoring along quite nicely, then something just changes? You're not even sure what's changed. It just… has.

'What's the matter?' you ask your partner because, without wishing to state the obvious, it's always better to ask what's wrong rather than moon around *wondering* what's wrong, or asking your friends what's wrong, or reading the *Daily Mail* horoscope for hints.

Just ask.

In the best-case scenario, Partner A will take a deep breath, invite you to sit down and tell you, in an articulate and grown-up manner, that you make a smacking noise when you eat that turns their stomach, and that their most exciting fantasies now only involve one person... You're being dumped.

But there's the thing. However harsh the character assassination gets, at least Partner A has had the good grace to sit you down, look you in the eye and do the deed. Big round of applause for Partner A. Now let's have a look at Partner B.

Grr, how we hate Partner B. 'What's the matter?' you ask them, and they grunt, shrug their shoulders and say, slightly defensively, 'Nothing.'

Sorry, but you're still being dumped. It's just that there are varying degrees of being dumped, and they range from very hideously unkind to the not quite so unkind. As the dumpee, it's your job to know the signs and act accordingly. Partner A's being all upfront and grown-up about it; no need to worry about them. But what about Partner B? They're trying a 'slow dump', that most protracted and sadistic of all dumps...

Slow Dumping – Know the Signs

No. 1

They stop returning your calls and there will always be a really 'good' reason why. Any reasonable person would understand the reason, but not you, because you're unreasonable.

- **Prognosis:** You're being dumped and – get this – they're going to make out it's your fault!

- **Counter-action:** Chuck them first, citing failure to correctly maintain and use telephonic apparatus. In other words, you don't want to go out with someone who's too stupid to access their voicemails/charge their handset/put credit on their phone.

No. 2

They become silent and withdrawn, sighing a lot, curling their lip when you ask them a question, making exasperated sounds at the simplest suggestion. They won't engage in *any* argument (map-reading, parking, politics, religion, bum is/is not big and so on), and they look distracted whenever you speak.

- **Prognosis:** You're being dumped, but they're hoping you're going to get so fed up with their adolescent behaviour that you'll dump them first, but only after you've surrendered every ounce of self-respect trying to save what you thought was a great relationship.

- **Counter-action:** They want to be dumped, so don't give them the satisfaction. Why not just break off all contact? It suits them now, sure, but you can guarantee that one day –

maybe not today, not tomorrow, but soon and for the rest of their lives – they'll wonder why you suddenly lost interest, and in some trivial way you will have triumphed. Ha!

No. 3

They tell you they've been missing their friends, and want to spend more time with them.

- **Prognosis:** Either you're being dumped or – worse, much worse – they're taking the first step on a road which begins with them wanting to see more of their mates. This moves on to them demanding to see their mates all weekend, to promising to come round after closing time but never actually appearing, to a 'friendship' with a member of the bar staff and, finally, to the two of you being pulled apart by security on *Trisha*.

- **Counter-action:** As anyone who recognizes a decent music score when they hear one knows, the hills are alive. So run to them.

No. 4

They tell you things are moving too quickly for them, and they want to take things a bit easier.

- **Prognosis:** As Yoda would say: dumped you are being. But it's the kind of dumping where they're going to keep you around for a while, just to have something warm to do with their private parts.

- **Counter-action:** Depends on you. Once you've sussed that they're not in it for the long haul, do you really want to stick around and enjoy the merciful delights of their bedroom, or move on to greener pastures? Whatever you do, though, don't hang on thinking you'll change their mind. There's not a hope in hell.

However it happens, here's the thing: you have to handle it. Part of doing that is just being philosophical about the whole episode. People split up all the time; that's how most relationships end. You know all those blisteringly happy couples you suddenly see around you? One day they may well feel just as you are feeling right now – just as soon as Derek goes one step too far with a lap dancer at Spearmint Rhino, or Fiona decides she'd really rather be with Paul from Human Resources, or Bill announces he wants to 'experiment' with Ben. People split up or they die. And hey, at least you didn't die.

Not that this helps in the white heat of rejection, of course. You can't sleep; you are a loser; people keep telling you that there are plenty more fish in the sea. You feel like an ugly, smelly, boring, overweight and badly dressed carcass.

You're not thinking straight. You are in shock. So, let's do some of that straight thinking for you:

10 Commandments of Being Dumped
(actually 11, but who's counting?)

I will remember that we are all universal losers Yes, because unless you're 92 and sitting by your loved one's side as they slip gently away, you're going to chuck or get chucked. It's a fact of life, like spots and tax.

I will not call them Okay, you might have to. There may be certain things you have to sort out. But not at 2am. And not when you've been drinking. And not 'to talk about things', or to ask stupid questions like 'Have you got my dry-cleaning ticket?' when they know damn well you haven't been to the dry-cleaners since forever.

I will not email them See above, mainly. However, preparing an email *can* be really therapeutic. Whatever you do, though, do *not* put anything in the 'to' field while preparing this letter. Write it, save it, amend it, but don't send it. If you do, you will instantly regret it. You will want to unsend it so badly that you would cheerfully gnaw through the telephone cable if you thought that would stop it going. So, don't.

After a while you will find that you don't need to send it anyway.

I will not go over to their house See above to the power of a zillion. You go round to their house and you are relationship pâté. Don't even think about going round to their house. Don't even think about *thinking* about going round to their house. Be assured that whatever you say will look at best pitiful and at worse like you're an axe murderer.

I have more in my life than my ex Believe it or not, breaking up gets easier the older you get. When you're 18, what else do you have to worry about but the right jeans to wear? Remember how simple it all was? By the time you've started work you've got more going on, and those responsibilities keep mounting: career path, mortgage, bills, MOTs. Pretty soon you'll hardly notice your partner has gone.

(But I don't have more in my life than my ex...) Then you need to work on that. And here's your chance. Without that deadbeat hanging around you can concentrate on work, get a new flat and do it up, pursue an interest, go dancing, get drunk, wake up hungover and rent exactly the comfort film you want. Cripes, we're getting jealous just thinking about it.

I will remember that other universal losers have been there before … so even though it's really getting on your nerves when they say, 'There are plenty more fish in the sea,' they're saying that because they've earned their getting-chucked Blue Peter badge. They've been there before, and they know that if you were thinking straight, you'd know it too. But you're not, so you need a little help, hence the fish thing. When the boot's on the other foot, you'll understand…

I will not immediately jump into bed with someone wildly unsuitable in the mistaken belief that my ex will be consumed with jealousy and want to get back with me Because they won't, and you'll feel mighty stupid asking a 20-year-old pharmacist about that itchy rash on your bits and pieces.

I will get back in the saddle So to speak. Listen, you're single. Do you have any idea how many people stuck in relationships in dullsville would *love* to be single? Being single rocks. It's a life of endless opportunity and possibility, and you owe it to yourself to get out there and enjoy it.

I will not become bitter and twisted Because if you do then before you know it you'll be shouting at passers-by from your park bench, fingerless gloves gripping a tin of super-strength cider and it's not a good look, so smile and pretend you still love the world. After all, it's nearly Christmas…

I will make myself feel better by telling myself I was never in love in the first place Maybe – just maybe – it is not your heart but your ego that has been smashed with a hammer. Are you gutted because you were genuinely in love or because, like everybody else, you hate being dumped from a great height?

Chucking Hell

It's horrible having to dump someone, and more than a little bit frightening. What if you regret it after the deed is done? Depending on the length of the relationship, you're lobbing a fairly large hand grenade into their life. The majority of us (around 99.9 per cent of us, in fact) will never kill anyone or commit any kind of violent crime. Most of us will probably never sack anyone, so finishing with someone is about as nasty as it gets. How do you do it? Well, er… you dodge, you fib or, if things have got fairly serious, then you tell the truth. Like this…

The Two-date Dumping Plan

Keyword: dodge If you need to dump somebody after two dates, well, it's not really dumping is it? Call it a tactical withdrawal. The best thing to do in this instance is politely say that you don't think this is going anywhere and then start not returning calls and texts; they should get the message. If they refuse to twig and they keep calling – with increasingly urgent declarations of undying love – you might want to think about leaving the country. You've got yourself a weirdo.

The Four-date Dumping Plan

Keyword: fib It took four dates to work out that Cupid had not only missed, but probably never even bothered firing to save on ammo. Now you've got to get creative. This involves – sorry – lying. Either tell them that you don't want to date at the moment or, better, bring a fictional ex back into the frame. The beginning of any new relationship is always haunted by the spectre of the last relationship, so they'll probably understand. If they don't, it means that they've never, ever got back with an ex. Which means they're a weirdo, and once again you may want to consider leaving the country.

The Five-date and Over Dumping Plan

Keyword: honesty Okay, now we're talking more serious stuff. The chances are you've actually slept with this person. You may even have said 'stuff'. It's got heavy. You think you're going to have to be Houdini to get out of this one. Well, if you've read the beginning of this chapter you'll remember Partner A. This was the partner who sits down and tells you honestly and directly that it's over. In actual fact, what this situation calls for is a subtle, sympathetic touch. Nobody wants to be told that the white stuff which forms in the corner of their mouth is repulsive. Nobody needs to hear that they cannot dress for shit. Remember, if you start slinging crap, the chances are they'll start slinging it back, and before you know it there'll be websites in your honour. Just be general, vague, nice.

The Russian Roulette Dump

The Russian roulette of dumping someone is to finish with them, telling them that you love them *too* much. Sounds risky, doesn't it? That's because it is. But if you get away with it you can end up dumping someone and not feeling bad. Result.

Of course, if it doesn't work, you could end up getting married to someone you really hate and having kids. But that's why we call it the Russian roulette dump.

So, now you've done it. What next? Prepare to do some grieving of your own for a start. You may feel relieved that you've finally got rid of your partner, but get set for some regrets, too. Chances are you'll also find that you've just given the heave-ho to the one person you'd want to share those feelings with. Your sense of loss may not be as acute as theirs, but more than likely it'll still make its presence felt, and you'll have doubts, questions…

The $64,000 Questions
(that's about £33,000 in sterling)

- **Should we be friends?** No. Certainly not yet. When you're being Partner A and you're sitting down with your soon-to-be ex and being – remember – gentle with your letdowns, please don't utter any sentence that includes the words 'we can still be' and 'friends', or any variation thereof. There's a good reason for this. First, you're telling porkies. You don't like this person all that much; you want them out of your life. The absolute last thing you need is them reminding you that you wanted to be friends, because then you've effectively got to dump them all over again, this time as a friend – and we'd need a whole new chapter to cover that.

- **Should we have one last shag, for old time's sake?** Probably not. Tempting as it is, that one last shag could be like a lovely comfy cat that's really nice to stroke in front of the fire, and feels so nice and warm and familiar… and then turns round and bites you. They're going to go for it, of course, but you probably shouldn't, although looking sorely tempted would probably be the polite thing to do in this instance.

- **What if they ask really politely?** Oh, go on then. But don't say we didn't warn you.

- **Should we get back together?** That depends, and a lot of it depends on why you dumped this person in the first place. If you chucked them because they were needy and insecure, the chances are that the experience of being dumped won't have helped fix that particular flaw – and you'll be saddled with a paranoid limpet whom you can't dump a second time for fear they will end it all (and you liked their Mum). But turn that on its head. What if you decided to kick this person into touch because they were complacent and took you for granted? In this instance, a good dose of getting chucked might be just what they need. The scales will fall from their eyes and (after a period of wooing you back, naturally) they'll be treating you with the 'rispeck' you deserve. Maybe. Or maybe not. Maybe they'll woo you, win you, then treat you like shit for another six months and you'll have to dump them, again. So, should you get back together? It's a judgment call. Yours.

- **Should I get closure?** What are you? A character in a Woody Allen movie?

Lastly, it's worth remembering that the person you've just dumped will look fantastic the next time you see them. That's nature's way of compensating them for their loss. There will also come a time when you'll see them with somebody else and they will cease being yours. You'd better get used to that. And now – really finally – use this experience. Whether you were the dumper or the dumpee, try and learn from it. Oh, and the next person you meet – ask them how their last relationship ended. If they tell you it was because they wanted to spend more time with their friends – then run.

Chapter Twenty-one

So, You're Single Again

it's not that bad, is it?

Oops. One moment it's hearts and flowers and day trips to Ann Summers for saucy underwear and flavoured lubricant. The next, you're working your way through a family-size box of Kleenex and your mother's worried you're not eating properly: the hearts were broken ones, the flowers stinging nettles; everybody in Ann Summers is having a better time than you...

Or are they?

The Bonus Features of Single Life

You Can Go Out After Work When You Want to

And you can do it without having to ring your partner first, 'just to check it's okay', and then endure a slightly tetchy conversation during which they say, 'I thought you said you were tired,' or, 'But you're going out tomorrow night...' which ends with you promising to have just one drink, which you don't really enjoy, knowing it's the only one you can have. Then, when you get home you get a frosty reception that completely cancels out any meagre pleasure the drink may have given you. Meanwhile, your friends from work are clearly getting dug in for a big night out, and tomorrow they'll all have hangovers and be slightly noisy and you'll feel excluded, knowing that you'd have stayed with them if you'd been single.

But, hey, you are single now, so the next round is yours...

You Can Sleep When and How You Want to

Because that snoring wildebeest who used to lie next to you has at last gone, so not only can you bin the earplugs, but you can lie any way you want.

You Can Make Your Own Tea

You can make yourself the simple drink you like without also having to make your partner the fiddly, complicated drink they prefer.

When it comes to tea you're not a fusspot, are you? You like a nice cup of builder's, no sugar, splash of milk, pretty much as it comes. Partners, on the other hand, always have to be different. *Always*. It's practically the law. They'll insist on some exotic blend of tea you'd never heard of previously. You'll need to follow precise instructions regarding brewing times, adding milk and so on, and it will need to be served in their 'special' mug. Put simply: your tea takes 30 seconds to make; theirs takes half an hour.

You Can Stop Pretending to Like...

James Blunt/*Grease*/The Fall or whatever other musical living death you were forced to put up with morning, noon and night. Because that was getting really very tiresome, wasn't it?

You Don't Have to Be Part of 'a Couple'

Let's face it: couples can be fairly nauseating at the best of times. Recognize any of these? Or, worse, were you actually *in* one of these...

- **The power couple** He drives a performance car (and, yes, he actually says the word 'performance' when he refers to his car – or 'her' as he will call it). Meanwhile, the female half of the couple plays tennis, knows where you bought the clothes you're wearing, and either has a high-flying career or has recently given one up to do something beneficial for mankind that will involve badgering you for donations and sponsorship money on a fortnightly basis.

  They turn up to events wearing perfectly co-ordinated clothes and have been known to perform choreographed dance routines. They commission Christmas cards to show off their house, their children or just their own beautifully defined cheekbones. They personalize these cards with your name and impersonalize them by popping in a 'round robin' letter, which tells everyone they have ever met that a knighthood is in the offing, their kids are going to the Sorbonne, and brother Jimmy has just received a Nobel Peace Prize.

  Their parties feature ice sculptures, sparkly bits sprinkled on the tables, and guests with straightened hair. If you suspect you are at a power-couple party, find a sofa – their sofas are really, really strange and can vary from Aztec Mexican inlaid wood to aquamarine leather. If the sofa is not obviously odd, try the bathroom next – if you find expensive cosmetics on display, fully charged ultrasound toothbrushes, a monogram or fleur-de-lys on a towel and the room seems to be 'scented', you can confirm your couple type. There may be a performance car magazine by the loo. Game over.

- **The lifestyle couple** He goes to gigs. She doesn't like pets. Their parties will be dinner parties. And you will eat well at their pad as they know their frittata from their fish fingers. You will probably stay over, too; they are good people to spend a Sunday with because you'll get brunch and watch a decent movie. On the other hand, they can be complete tightwads as they're always saving for their next holiday, most likely in Cuba. Ugh.

- **The best friend couple** These two are so called because they're best mates, which makes them a great couple. They're fun – they do fun things, they share their fun friends and the fun contents of their fun fridge. They don't really plan parties, but most weekends will become one. They embrace a lot, and give each other secret smiles. If you weren't depressed about being single before meeting this pair you certainly will be afterwards. Hurl.

- **The shag-a-lots** The shag-a-lot couple are a 24-hour, seven-day-a-week wince-a-thon. They let you know (when you least expect it) that they always walk around the house naked, share regular baths together and 'enjoy one another' in the bedroom on a daily – nay hourly – basis. Their parties are always very drunken affairs; the next day you won't be sure whether or not someone made a pass at you. They have erotic pictures all over the house, and they have tight bums. If they are a 'best friend couple' as well you are staring troo love in the face. Once again you'll be left feeling inadequate and desperately alone. You'll hate them.

- **The share-a-lots** This pair argue in front of you, tell you about their rubbish sex life, tell you where they are going wrong and where you should go right. You always know where you stand with a share-a-lot couple, and they will be constantly fixing you up with potential partners of your very own. Their gatherings are beers-in-the-bath and sausage roll affairs – conversation is the most impor- tant thing about this get-together. They can be a most affable breed – but need to get in touch with their inner child after a bottle of plonk, so you've got to be prepared to listen. And listen. And listen. Yawn.

- **The lovebirds** As Dorothy from Kansas would say, 'There's no place like home.' There is no place like home – and the lovebirds are at theirs. That's why you haven't seen them for months on end. Be happy for them and hope they emerge engaged before the wind picks up. Smile, through gritted teeth.

No More Worrying that They Might Find Out...

that you snogged that person from sales at the last Christmas party. It was a one-off. You were drunk; so were they. You kissed. Yes, there was face action. Worse, there were one or two witnesses, and ever since you've been bricking your britches that your partner will learn of your minor indiscretion. But now you're single *it doesn't matter* if they find out. Hell, why not just go ahead and tell them yourself?

You'll Drive How You Like, Thanks

You were driving perfectly safely for years before you met your ex. Hey, you could even manage roundabouts without their help. You'll be driving perfectly safely when they're gone. Weird, that.

You Don't Have to Keep Quiet about Hating Their Mum

Wasn't she a bitch? The way she used to smile at you immediately prior to saying something vile like, 'Is your hair naturally that colour?' Or, 'That's a very *interesting* top.' Well, now you can tell your partner exactly what you thought of their horror of a parent. Tell the world if you like. Go on, you have our blessing.

(One note of caution, on this, though: make sure you don't
ever want to revisit this relationship, as slagging off their
mother takes a great deal of undoing.)

You Can Start Leading
Your Friends Astray

For the duration of your relationship you've had to put up
with your pals egging you on to have 'just one more drink', or
to go clubbing when you'd promised to be home at 8pm and
to go to your partner's big family event the next day. (A christening. It's always a christening.) You, being both a good
friend and a good partner, have tried unsuccessfully to make
this situation work and ended up pleasing neither party. Your
partner has resented your nights out, while your friends have
felt neglected. Guess what? It's time to wave bye-bye to Mr
and Mrs Guilty. You're the free agent now, and you can start
applying the thumbscrews to those very same friends. All
together now, 'Come on, just *one more drink*...'

No More Fighting over the Best
Sweets in a Box of Quality Street

How come there are only toffee ones left? Did you eat all the
strawberry fondants? Did you? *Did you?* (Repeat till fade.)

You Won't Spend Half Your Life Texting

You know what it's like. You're in the middle of an important business meeting or sitting on the train or up a mountain or on the toilet and – *bing* – a text arrives from your beloved. 'I love you,' it says, 'and can you pop to Marks on the way back for some garlic bread?'

Guh.

Now you've got to drop whatever you were doing and text back straight away. Woe betide you if you don't.

You Don't Need to Puzzle over Emails, Wondering What They Really Mean

Normally they end their emails with four little kisses, like this: 'xxxx', but on this particular occasion they've only put three little kisses, like this: 'xxx'. Does that mean they love you one kiss less? Are they cooling off? How come they love you one kiss less all of a sudden? What is their problem? *What is their bloody problem?*

Yes, you can say goodbye to all of that. Next time you get an email from them it won't have any kisses. They probably won't even put your name at the top of it. It'll just say, 'Your car tax thingy turned up. Shall I forward it?' And you'll reply, 'Yes, thanks, if you would,' and all will be right with the world.

Flirting Now Comes Guilt-free

And you don't have to be surreptitious when you want to check somebody out in the supermarket. Because that was getting tiresome too, wasn't it? If there's somebody on the telly and you think they look pretty hot you should be able to think it – and possibly even say it – without being accused of infidelity and getting a plate thrown at your head. Now you can fancy who you want and flirt with anyone you like, no comebacks. The freedom!

You Can Be Yourself

You can wear all of those clothes that they hated but you secretly loved. You'll grow your hair if that's what you've always wanted to do. You can have the odd fag when you're pissed without them complaining about the smell, watching whatever you want on the telly...

And Finally, the Very Best Things about Being Single...

You are no longer wasting your time with that loser...

You can start dating...

You get to read this book all over again and meet great new people in weird places and go out on dates and have a brilliant laugh, and meet even more great new people and have loads of snogs (and the rest!) and meet their friends and family and guess what?

We'll still be *dead* jealous.